Dear Bryony

Hope you enjoy the recipes!

Nourish & glow,

Marlen Wright xx

The Yoga Kitchen

The Yoga Kitchen

100 Easy Superfood Recipes

Marlien Wright

JACANA

To my Milla & Ava, who are always hungry, and inspire me to create recipes that are both healthy and yummy

Acknowledgements

A heartfelt thank you to Yoga, all my fabulous friends, and retreat participants over the years, who encouraged and inspired me to keep cooking and stay on my mat.

Thank you to Alex and Bruce from Atelier for letting me use their gorgeous lifestyle pictures of Swellendam and surrounds.

First published by Jacana Media (Pty) Ltd in 2016

10 Orange Street
Sunnyside
Auckland Park 2092
South Africa
+2711 628 3200
www.jacana.co.za

© Marlien Wright, 2016

All rights reserved.

ISBN 978-1-4314-2404-7

Design by Shawn Paikin
Photo contributors: Bruce Geils and Alex Hayn at
Atelier Design Studio www.atelier.co.za
Set in Bodoni Egyptian Pro 9.3/14pt
Printed and bound by Imago
Job no. 002696

See a complete list of Jacana titles at www.jacana.co.za

Contents

Introduction

Introduction

My *Yoga Kitchen* recipes, a celebration of nourishing wholefoods, will boost your immune system and enable you to reclaim the inherent power to heal yourselves of diet-related issues, thus forging new healthy habits.

There is a growing awareness that processed convenience food is damaging our health by depleting our body's gut flora, enzymes, minerals and vitamin stores, not to mention the fibre and phytonutrients we miss out on, which are only available from whole foods. This book provides the tools and knowledge to return to the kitchen, re-learning the skills to cook delicious and nourishing meals we can share with our loved ones. After all, cooking from scratch is a simple, yet profound, task that makes us feel needed and connected to one another.

Any healthy dish can become delicious if paired with the right ingredients and sauces. Every recipe in this book is designed to enhance your digestion, boost energy levels, and make you look and feel your best.

All my *Yoga Kitchen* recipes are easy to prepare and nutritious, demonstrating that healthy food choices can be delicious too. Each recipe also has a summary attached that highlights the main ingredients' health benefits and nutritional content.

Other helpful tools include:

· My *Yoga Kitchen* food philosophy, how to avoid toxins in foods, essential pantry ingredients, and cooking tips and tools.

· A–Z Guide of the sources and roles of vitamins, minerals and other essential nutrients for a closer look into the nutrition of whole foods.

· My *Yoga Kitchen* 21-day reboot meal plan.

· Traditional food-preserving and cooking methods that will transform your health (see page 38)

Yoga Kitchen Food Philosophy

Food combining

All the recipes in this book adhere to food-combining rules. Food combining means that you do not eat animal protein and carbohydrates (starches) in the same meal. So, when eating fish or meat, you can combine it only with watery vegetables like peppers, aubergines, salad leaves, tomatoes, cucumbers, asparagus, broccoli, cauliflower, cabbage, etc. When eating a carbohydrate-based meal you can combine it with watery vegetables and starchy vegetables, as well as plant-based protein sources like beans, lentils, nuts, quinoa and tofu.

Food combining creates an alkaline environment in the body, hugely important for good health and immunity. Food combining also makes it easier for your body to absorb nutrients from food and assist in excellent digestion (you will find that bloating and acid reflux disappears).

Vegan/Vegetarian versus Paleo diet

Both these lifestyle diets can be very beneficial from a health point of view. It really depends on the individual, their beliefs and other factors such as lifestyle, blood type, digestive system, etc. What we should remember though is that vitamin B12 is only available from animal products like meat and dairy, and this vitamin fulfils hugely important roles in the body like helping the blood carry oxygen, which is essential for energy production, and is extremely important for nerve function. If you choose to become a vegan (vegetarians can get B12 from dairy and eggs), make sure you are supplementing with B12.

Fats

Fat is an essential nutrient that we have shunned for too long. It is important for our brain health and many other functions in the body. Choosing healthy fats is key and as with everything else, fats should also be used in moderation.

Use pasture-fed, cow's milk butter: it is unprocessed and contains only minimal ingredients, cream and salt. It is easy to make butter at home: simply buy pasture-fed, free-range or organic cream and churn until it turns into butter – you can add pink salt if you wish.

Avoid margarine and olive oil spreads; they are highly processed and classified as trans fats.

Coconut oil

Coconut oil is best for cooking as it can withstand higher temperatures without being damaged. It has some amazing health benefits too: 50% of coconut oil is lauric acid, which is rarely found in nature. Your body converts lauric acid into monolaurin, a monoglyceride that has the ability to destroy lipid-coated viruses like herpes and other harmful microbes.

Coconut oil is comprised of medium-chain fatty acids that are easily digested, and gets immediately converted into energy by your liver, rather than being stored as fat.

Use coconut oil to make 'bullet-proof' coffee before exercise.

Olive oil

Olive oil should be used raw, in other words use it only in salad dressings, or to drizzle over food that has been taken off the heat and slightly cooled, just before serving. Olive oil should never be used to cook with as it cannot withstand high temperatures and becomes toxic. When selecting olive oil choose a cold-pressed oil to ensure that all vital nutrients are still intact. Olive oil is rich in antioxidants and good fats.

Soaking nuts, seeds & grains

Nuts, seeds and grains are packed with highly beneficial nutrients. However, it is a good idea to soak them before eating them which helps break down anti-nutrients (substances that interfere with the body's ability to absorb nutrients) and allows optimal absorption of the beneficial nutrients. Soak them in warm water for 7–24 hours (so overnight works well if you are using them the next day).

Avoiding toxins in food

Avoid pesticides

Buy organic produce, but if you can't get hold of organic produce then always wash vegetables thoroughly, using a vegetable brush, and peel them where necessary. Only buy whole unprocessed vegetables, prepping them yourself at home.

Tinned food

Choose beans or tomatoes packed in BPA-free tins.

Using passata (pulped tomatoes without pips or skin) in a glass jar or bottle is a much better and healthier alternative to tinned tomatoes. Beans are a simple affair to cook at home if you get around to soaking them overnight.

Preservatives & additives

It is best to always use fresh produce and unpreserved ingredients. Be wary of long lists of ingredients with names you don't recognise, or products your great granny wouldn't recognise. Such products are full of unnecessary additives that are harmful to your health. Only visit the vegetable, egg, dried wholegrain and meat isles in the supermarket, or even better, shop at a farmers' market for your weekly groceries.

Avoid processed food

It often has very little nutrition and is loaded with refined white flour and sugar, both of which are detrimental to your health. If time is an issue, use the **21-day Yoga Kitchen Meal Plan** to buy and prepare meals ahead from scratch. It is helpful to double up recipes for two nights or lunches ahead.

Avoid plastic/BPA

Avois using or buying food in plastic & polystyrene packaging, use glass or stainless steel containers to store food in.

The microwave

I am not a fan – microwaves simply destroy too many nutrients in food. I use a small sauce pan to heat leftover soups or food on the hob. Try and phase yours out as much as possible.

Essential salt

Use Himalayan pink salt instead of ordinary table salt, or sea, or rock salt. Himalayan salt is not processed – it is hand mined and hand washed, therefore it retains all of its healthy minerals that are so important for bone health. It also adds a delicious flavour to food.

Why pasture-raised meat and poultry is better

For the sake of our precious planet, as well as your own health, it is essential that we choose organic or pasture-raised/grass-fed meat and poultry. Pasture-raised meat is far higher in good fats like omega-3 fatty acids. It is also important that meat is hormone and antibiotic-treatment free, as those 'added ingredients' to your diet cause havoc in your body. Steer well clear of the cheaper grain-fed beef and chicken products. It is far better to eat less meat, finding the protein we need in plant-based sources like quinoa, beans, lentils, nuts and seeds like chia and hemp seeds, or tempeh. Fish should be ethically caught and steer clear of the larger breeds or farmed fish due to the dangerous mercury content.

Choose non-GMO

There is a whole host of reasons why GMO foods are not good for you. GMO foods can contain allergens as they are gene-altered while GM crops contain a pesticide-resistant gene, which means they can be sprayed heavily with pesticides. This increases heavy pesticide exposure for humans, as well as farm animals. But the most worrisome element of consuming GMO foods is the effect on gene expression in humans, where genes can be either be suppressed or overexpressed, causing a wide variety of results in our bodies. Many researchers suspect the rise in cancer to be one of these results. Do your own reading and research and perhaps avoid GMO wherever you can, choosing organic where possible. Look out for a non-GMO sticker or label on the packaging; if there is no clear indication that the product is non-GMO, then you can safely assume that some or all ingredients are of GMO origin.

Essential tools

I am quite certain I wouldn't be able to live without the following kitchen paraphernalia:

· Hand blender for smoothies and soups; I use a 400w model.

· Food processor for shredding, making nut butters, pestos and pastes.

· Cast-iron cooking skillet or deep pan. Cast iron is by far the healthiest cooking material to use as they allow the safest 'non-stick' cooking around. You can also easily transfer a cast-iron pot from the stove top to the oven, not to mention that they last forever and can even be passed on to your children.

· Small oven for baking potatoes and sweet potatoes, and roasting veggies. Using a small, fast-heating little oven saves a huge amount of electricity.

· Sharp knives

· Good garlic crusher

· Sharp vegetable peeler that can peel butternut and fruit alike

· Silicon spatula and wooden spoons

· At least one large mixing bowl

· Large salad spinner

· Measuring jug, cups and spoons

Yoga Kitchen pantry essentials

Grains

Brown basmati rice
Course polenta
Gluten-free rolled oats
Pearled barley
Quinoa (technically a seed)

Pulses & Legumes

Split red lentils
Split peas (for vegetable soups)
Chickpeas
Black beans
Cannellini beans
Kidney beans

Flours

Chickpea (chana) flour
Almond flour
Coconut flour
Stone-ground wheat flour (non-GMO)

Nuts & Seeds (raw)

Almonds
Cashews
Walnuts
Sesame seeds (hulled)
Chia seeds
Pumpkin seeds
Hemp seeds
Sunflower seeds

Oils & Vinegars

Cold-pressed olive oil
Cold-pressed coconut oil (deodorised)
Raw apple cider vinegar
White wine vinegar

Sauces, Pastes & Nut Butters

Red curry paste
Tomato paste
Tahini
Peanut butter (non-GMO)
Cashew or almond butter

Miscellaneous

Passata in glass jars (pulped tomatoes)
Coconut cream and milk
Cacao powder
Non-GMO, gluten-free vegetable stock
Desiccated coconut
Himalayan (pink) salt
Almond milk

Dried Herbs & Spices

Thyme
Oregano
Mixed herbs
Mint

Ground spices:
Turmeric
Cumin
Coriander
Sweet paprika
Fennel
Cinnamon
All spice
Masala (Rajah brand–mild)
Garam masala
Sumac

Whole spices:
Cumin seeds
Whole pepper corns
Caraway seeds
Fennel seeds
Mustard seeds
Cloves
Cardamom
Bay leaves
Curry leaves
Star anise
Vanilla pods

The A–Z of Essential Vitamins and Minerals

Vitamin A

Important for healthy skin and vision, it protects against infections and many types of cancer. Vitamin A is an important antioxidant and immune booster.

Sources: carrots, sweet potatoes, watercress, mangoes, pumpkins, cabbage, apricots, tomatoes and broccoli

Vitamin B1 (thiamine)

Essential for energy production, brain function and digestion. Assists the body in making use of protein.

Sources: asparagus, peas, cauliflower, courgettes, Brussels sprouts and lamb

Vitamin B2 (riboflavin)

B2 assists in turning fats, sugar and protein into energy. Repairs and maintains healthy skin, helps to regulate body acidity, and is important for hair, nail and eye health.

Sources: wheat germ, asparagus, mushrooms, broccoli, pumpkin and watercress

Vitamin B3 (niacin)

Essential for energy production, brain function and healthy skin, balances blood sugar and lowers cholesterol. Reduces inflammation and improves digestion.

Sources: mushrooms, tomatoes, courgettes, whole wheat, asparagus, cauliflower, chicken, mackerel and salmon

Vitamin B5

Important for energy production, controls fat metabolism, essential for brain and nerve health. Helps make anti-stress hormones and helps maintain healthy skin and hair.

Sources: mushrooms, lentils, avocado, alfalfa sprouts, whole wheat, strawberries, watercress, tomatoes, cabbage and celery

Vitamin B6 (pyridoxine)

B6 is essential for the utilising and digestion of protein. It is also important for healthy brain function and hormone production. Helps balance sex hormones, and is a natural anti-depressant and diuretic. Helps control allergic reactions.

Sources: wheat germ, eggs, watercress, cauliflower, bananas, red kidney beans, squash, tuna, salmon and Brussels sprouts

Vitamin B12 (cyanocobalamin)

Essential for energy production and very important for bone health. B12 is also needed for making use of protein and the synthesis of DNA, to assist blood to transport oxygen, and is essential for good nerve health.

Sources: sardines, oysters, cottage cheese, tuna, shrimp, free-range eggs, lamb, grass-fed beef and beef liver, raw milk and chicken

Folic Acid

Critical during pregnancy for development of brain and nerves, essential for brain and nerve function, needed for utilising protein and red blood cell formation.

Sources: wheat germ, cooked lentils, spinach, sprouts, broccoli, peanuts, cauliflower, asparagus, cashew nuts, avocados and sesame seeds

Biotin

Important during childhood, helps the body use essential fats and assists in promoting healthy hair, skin and nails.

Sources: free-range eggs, almonds, herrings, oysters, sweet corn, watermelon

Vitamin C (ascorbic acid)

Very important for heart health, strengthens immune system, essential free radical-fighting antioxidant, makes collagen, keeping bones, skin and joints firm and strong. Detoxifies pollutants and may lower blood pressure and keep arteries flexible. Helps make anti-stress hormones and turns food into energy.

Sources: peppers, broccoli, watercress, papaya, chilli peppers, Brussels sprouts, tomatoes, sweet potatoes, strawberries, lemons, peas, tomatoes, kiwi fruit, melons, oranges and grapefruit, kale

Vitamin D

Vitamin D is involved in the biomechanical cellular machinery of all the cells and tissues in your body. When you are deficient, your entire body will struggle to function optimally. Vitamin D is also important for maintaining strong and healthy bones by retaining calcium.

Sources: herrings, mackerel, salmon, sardines, oysters, cottage cheese and eggs

Vitamin E (d-alpha tocopherol)

Very important antioxidant that protects cells from damage, including against cancer, helps body use oxygen, prevents blood clots, thrombosis, improves wound healing and fertility, very good for skin health. It may also be useful in the treatment of obesity and fatty liver disease.

Sources: almonds, walnuts, sunflower seeds, sesame seeds, wheat germ, beans, peanuts, peas, spinach, broccoli, tuna, sardines and salmon

Vitamin K (phylloquinone)

Controls blood clotting, plays an important role in bone health. Assists with heart disease prevention and reduces neural damage as well as neutralises free radical damage.

Sources: cauliflower, Brussels sprouts, broccoli, lettuce, cabbage, beans, watercress, potatoes, asparagus, tomatoes and peas, fermented vegetables and soya

Calcium

Promotes a healthy heart, clots blood, promotes healthy nerves, contracts muscles and improves skin, bone and teeth health, relieves aching muscles and bones, maintains the correct acid and alkaline balance, reduces menstrual cramps and tremors.

Sources: almonds, Swiss cheese, brewer's yeast, parsley, cooked dried beans and pumpkin seeds

Chromium

Forms part of the glucose tolerance factor. To balance blood sugar, helps to normalise hunger and reduce cravings.

Sources: brewer's yeast, rye, wheat germ, oysters, eggs, apples, parsnips and chicken

Iron

As a compound of haemoglobin, iron transports oxygen and carbon dioxide to and from cells. It is a component of enzymes, and is vital for energy production.

Sources: pumpkin seeds, parsley, cashew nuts, sesame seeds, Brazil nuts, cooked dried beans, pecans, walnuts, lentils, spirulina, spinach and lamb kidney

Magnesium

Strengthens bones and teeth, promotes healthy muscles by helping them to relax, so important to assist with PMS, important for heart muscles and nervous system, essential for energy production, enzymatic co-factor.

Sources: wheat germ, almonds, cashew nuts, brewer's yeast, buckwheat flour, Brazil nuts, peanuts, pecan nuts, cooked beans, peas, potato skin, raisins and crab meat

Manganese

Helps to form healthy bones, cartilage, tissues and nerves, activates more than twenty enzymes, including an antioxidant enzyme system. Stabilises blood sugar, promotes healthy DNA and RNA, essential for reproduction and red blood synthesis, important for insulin production, reduces cell damage, required for brain function.

Sources: beetroot, grapes, strawberries, oats, watercress, pineapple, okra, endive, blackberries, raspberries and lettuce

Molybdenum

Assists the body in getting rid of protein-breakdown products, e.g. uric acid. Strengthens teeth. Detoxifies the body from free radicals, petrochemicals and sulphites.

Sources: tomatoes, wheat germ, lamb, lentils and beans

Phosphorus

Forms and maintains bones and teeth, needed for milk secretion, builds muscle tissue, is a component of DNA and RNA. Helps maintain the pH of the body, aids in metabolism and energy production.

Sources: present in almost all foods

Potassium

Enables nutrients to move into and out of cells. Promotes healthy nerves and muscles, maintains fluid balance in the body. Relaxes muscles, helps secretion of insulin for blood-sugar control to produce constant energy. Maintains heart function and stimulates gut movement.

Sources: molasses, parsley, watercress, radishes, bananas, pumpkin, coconut, endive, celery, mushrooms, cabbage and cauliflower

Selenium

Potent antioxidant that protects against free radicals and carcinogens. Reduces inflammation, stimulates immune system to fight infections. Needed for metabolism and a healthy heart.

Sources: tuna, Brazil nuts, oysters, herrings, mushrooms, molasses, courgettes, cabbage, chicken and cottage cheese

Sodium

Maintains body's water balance preventing dehydration. Helps nerve function, used in muscle contraction including heart muscle. Helps move nutrients into cells.

Sources: plentiful in most foods, but try olives, sauerkraut, miso paste, celery, cabbage, watercress and kidney beans, for additional benefits

Zinc

Component of over 200 enzymes in the body, component of DNA and RNA, essential for growth and important for healing, controls hormones which are messengers from organs such as testes and ovaries, promotes a healthy nervous system and brain especially in a foetus. Aids bone and teeth formation, essential for constant energy.

Sources: oysters, dry split peas, peanuts, almonds, pecan nuts, Brazil nuts, eggs, green peas, whole wheat, oats

Essential oils

Omega-3 Fatty Acids

Promotes a healthy heart, thins the blood, preventing blood clots, reduces inflammation, relieves depression and attention deficit disorder, hyperactivity and autism. Improves sleep, improves skin condition, helps balance hormones and reduces insulin resistance.

Sources: mackerel, tuna, salmon, sardines, chia seeds, flax seeds and sunflower seeds

Omega-6 Fatty Acids

Promotes a healthy heart, thins the blood, reduces inflammation, improves nervous system function, relieves depression and attention deficit disorder, hyperactivity and autism. Improves sleep, improves skin condition, helps balance hormones, and reduces insulin resistance.

Sources: safflower oil, cold-pressed sunflower oil, sunflower seeds, pumpkin seeds, walnuts, wheat germ and sesame seeds

Other important antioxidants

Bioflavonoids

Assists vitamin C to work and activate, strengthens capillaries, speeds up healing of wounds, sprains and muscle injuries, antioxidant, DNA and cell protection.

Sources: berries, cherries and citrus fruit

Choline

Helps break down fat in liver, facilitates movement of fats into cells and synthesis of cell membranes in the nervous system, and protects lungs.

Sources: lecithin, eggs, fish, liver, soya beans, peanuts, whole grains, nuts, pulses, citrus fruit, wheat germ, brewer's yeast

Co-enzyme Q10

Plays a central role in energy metabolism, improves heart function, helps to normalise blood pressure, increases exercise tolerance, antioxidant, boosts immunity.

Sources: sardines, mackerel, pork, spinach, sesame seeds, peanuts and walnuts

Inositol

Needed for cell growth, required by brain and spinal cord, and for formation of nerve sheath, mild tranquiliser, maintains healthy hair, reduces blood cholesterol.

Sources: pulses, lecithin, eggs, fish, liver, citrus fruits, melon, nuts wheat germ and brewer's yeast

Some real food 'supplements'

Do consider incorporating these into your diet as they are affordable and packed with nutrition:

- Brewer's yeast powder
- Wheat germ
- Green tea
- Cold-pressed oils
- Chia seeds
- Raw cacao (or at least 85%-cocoa dark chocolate)
- Raw apple cider vinegar
- Raw honey
- Wheatgrass powder

Yoga Kitchen 21-Day Reboot Plan

This eating plan is based on my *Yoga Kitchen* food philosophy which adheres to the food-combining rules and includes mainly plant-based wholefoods.

The benefits of eating a wide variety of plant-based wholefoods, combined in the correct way with good quality animal proteins, will allow your body to digest and assimilate nutrients from food optimally. It creates an alkaline environment, which is important for a healthy immune system, and arms you with all the fibre, vitamins, minerals and phytonutrients your body needs to function optimally, providing you with boundless energy and glowing skin. It can assist in alleviating allergies and digestive issues like bloating, indigestion and skin disorders. While following the reboot plan it is important to exclude all sugary drinks from your diet. Drink filtered water and herbal or green teas, and include no more than one sugar-free/sweetener-free coffee a day, adding almond or rice milk instead of cow's milk.

Drinking plenty of water is important, but stick to the following water rules:

· Don't drink water during or just after meals.

· Work towards drinking eight glasses of filtered water a day, consuming these 20 minutes or more before meals, or at least an hour after a meal.

This is a general plan and could need adjustments to meet different dietary needs and lifestyles.

Go to my www.yogakitchen.co.za to sign up for a personalised 21-day plan.

WEEK 1

Day 1
Breakfast: Turmeric Eggs
Lunch: Mexican Blackbean and Corn Salad
Dinner: Superfood Salmon Meal

Day 2
Breakfast: Glow smoothie
Lunch: Mexican Blackbean and Corn Salad
Dinner: Bazaar Ground Beef Curry with Cauli-rice

Day 3
Breakfast: Grain-free Granola
Lunch: Salad No-çoise
Dinner: Baked Tofu & Veggie Rice

Day 4
Breakfast: Super C Smoothie
Lunch: Leftover Baked Tofu & Veggie Rice
Dinner: Paleo Roast Chicken & Vegetable Roast

Day 5
Breakfast: Turmeric Eggs
Lunch: Rainbow Slaw and Quinoa
Dinner: Prawn and Avocado Boats

Day 6
Breakfast: Glow Smoothie
Lunch: Nachos Salad
Dinner: Steak with Homemade Mustard and a Glow Salad

Day 7
This is your rest day. Today you can eat anything you want for lunch and dinner but avoid sugar and refined foods made from white flour.

WEEK 2

Day 1

Breakfast: Glow Smoothie

Lunch: Quinoa with Roasted Vegetables & Wilted Spinach

Dinner: Hake with Pesto & Baby Tomatoes

Day 2

Breakfast: Mexican Eggs

Lunch: Hummus, Pumpkin Seeds and Carrots Salad Boats

Dinner: Stuffed Peppers

Day 3

Breakfast: Super C Smoothie

Lunch: Salad No-Çoise

Dinner: Mandarin Chicken Stir-fry

Day 4

Breakfast: Grain-free Granola

Lunch: Glow Bowl

Dinner: Bean Chilli with Quinoa

Day 5

Breakfast: Glow Smoothie, and Grain-free Granola as a midmorning snack

Lunch: Glow Bowl

Dinner: Greek Lamb Chops with Tzatziki and Greens

Day 6

Breakfast: Shakshuka

Lunch: Green Goddess Salad

Dinner: Lentil Shepherd's Pie

Day 7

This is your rest day. Today you can eat anything you want for lunch and dinner but avoid sugar and refined foods made from white flour.

WEEK 3

Day 1

Breakfast: Super C Smoothie

Lunch: Daily Detox Salad with a Baked Sweet Potato

Dinner: Superfood Salmon Meal

Day 2

Breakfast: Glow smoothie

Lunch: Rainbow Slaw with Quinoa

Dinner: Bone Broth Soup

Day 3

Breakfast: Super C Smoothie

Lunch: Salad No-Çoise

Dinner: Bone Broth Veggie Soup

Day 4

Breakfast: Glow Smoothie

Lunch: Buddha Bowl

Dinner: Bean Chilli with quinoa

Day 5

Breakfast: Grain-free Granola

Lunch: Buddha Bowl

Dinner: Shakshuka

Day 6

Breakfast: Super C Smoothie with some Granola & Tahini for a midday snack

Lunch: Green Goddess Salad

Dinner: Vegan Thai Red Curry with Quinoa

Day 7

This is your rest day, today you can anything you choose for lunch and dinner but avoid sugar and refined foods made from white flour.

Breaking
the Fast

Power Smoothies

Super C Smoothie Makes 1 large or 2 small smoothies

2 oranges, peeled
½ cup of mixed frozen berries
½ cup of papaya, peeled
Small knob of ginger, peeled & grated
1 tsp ground turmeric
1 tbsp chia seeds

Add all the ingredients to a blender jug, and then simply blend until you have a smooth texture.

Health benefits

Chia seeds are nutritional gold, as they are the single richest plant-based source of omega-3 fatty acids. Chia seeds are also loaded with protein, antioxidants and minerals.

Turmeric is a powerful anti-inflammatory which can help in the reduction of pain, fatigue, and the improving of mood and cognitive function. Curcumin, an element contained in turmeric, also helps stops the progression of cancer cells.

Orange and berries with their high doses in vitamin C promote collagen production, boost the immune system, and are powerful antioxidants. **Berries** and **papaya** are also a great sources of bioflavonoids that work in synergy with vitamin C, which accounts for their anti-infection properties.

Ginger is a good source of magnesium and potassium. It has other elements like gingerol which improves cardiovascular circulation, besides being well known to be a powerful natural remedy for nausea and gassiness/bloating.

Enzyme & Vitamin A Smoothie Makes 1 large or 2 small smoothies

⅓ cup of fresh pineapple
⅓ cup of papaya
⅓ cup of mango
¼ cup of hemp seeds

Add all the ingredients to a blender jug and simply blend until you have a smooth texture.

Health benefits

Enzymes are essential for good health as they assist in energy production, absorption of oxygen, fighting infections and healing wounds, reducing inflammation, getting nutrients into your cells, breaking down fats in the body, proper regulation of hormones and carrying toxins out of the body. **Papaya** and **pineapple** are both especially rich in enzymes.

All smoothies are gluten, grain & dairy free. Vegan and paleo friendly.

(continued on following page)

(Power Smoothies Continued)

Glow Smoothie Makes 1 large or 2 small smoothies

I try to have a green smoothie for breakfast at least 3–4 times a week to boost my immune system and to help keep my skin in a supple condition.

To make this smoothie even more glow-worthy add a scoop of powdered greens like wheatgrass or barley grass, which will add a super punch of chlorophyll, vitamins and minerals.

1 cup of baby spinach or kale, washed and dried
1 small avocado, peeled
1 small banana, peeled
1 kiwi, peeled
¼ cucumber
100 ml water or pure coconut water

Add all the ingredients to a blender jug, and then simply blend until you have a smooth texture.

Health benefits

Avocados have good fats, which will give you sustained energy throughout the morning. They are also rich in vitamin E, folic acid and antioxidants.

The **leafy greens** in this smoothie promote glowing health with huge amounts of phytonutrients, fibre, vitamin A, C, K as well as folic acid and potassium.

Post-Practice Protein Smoothie Makes 1 large or 2 small smoothies

1 cup of almond milk
1 ripe banana
8 raw almonds, soaked overnight
8 raw cashew nuts, soaked overnight
2 tbsp hemp seeds, soaked overnight
1 tsp cinnamon
1 tsp raw honey

Add all the ingredients to the blender jug, and then simply blend until you have a smooth texture. Remember that your nuts and seeds need to be soaked overnight to get a smooth texture.

Health benefits

Almonds are rich in vitamin E, omega-3 fatty acids, protein, manganese, zinc and calcium. I recommend soaking almonds overnight before use as this deactivates the enzyme-inhibiting compound found in their skin.

Cashews are high in magnesium, a mineral which most people are deficient in due to large-scale farming. Magnesium is involved in over 200 functions in our bodies. Cashews also contain vitamin E, copper, iron and selenium.

Bananas are high in potassium. An excellent prebiotic (food for good bacteria), they are also rich in folic acid and other antioxidants.

Raw, unprocessed honey has powerful antibacterial and anti-fungal properties as well as trace enzymes, minerals, vitamins and amino acids. It is one of nature's true healing gifts to us. Raw, locally produced honey can help relieve allergies and makes an excellent natural cough mixture if prepared properly on a low heat with lemon rind and juice.

4

Overnight Nuts & Seeds Power Oats Serves 2

Overnight Oats (also known as Bircher's Muesli) is the perfect summer alternative to hot porridge oats and a great breakfast on the run as all the work gets done the night before.

1 cup of gluten-free, non-GMO, rolled oats

⅓ cup of raw walnuts

2 tbsp chia seeds

1 tbsp hemp seeds

1 tsp good vanilla extract

1 tsp ground cinnamon

300 ml almond milk or filtered water

Chopped banana, raw honey and berries for serving

Add all the ingredients into a deep bowl, then mix well and cover with cling film. Pop it in the fridge overnight and serve this creamy delicious oats with raw honey, or real maple syrup for a vegan option. Garnish with banana and berries and enjoy.

Health benefits

The soluble fibre in **oats**, which captures bad cholesterol, makes it one of the most heart-healthy foods you can eat. Oats is a good source of manganese, molybdenum, phosphorus, biotin, magnesium, chromium and zinc (making this a great 'skin food'). Oats and cinnamon are also beneficial to diabetics as it helps stabilise blood sugar levels.

Hemp seeds, rich in omega-6 and -3 fatty acids, are essential for heart health and have important anti-inflammatory properties. Hemp seeds are also an excellent source of vitamin E and protein.

Chia seeds are nutritional gold as they are the richest plant-based source of omega-3 fatty acids. Chia seeds are also loaded with protein, antioxidants and minerals.

Walnuts can help reduce bad cholesterol, improve metabolism and aid in weight management. They also possess anti-inflammatory properties and can be a mood booster. Walnuts are also a great source of omega 3 fatty acids.

Gluten & dairy free. Vegan friendly.

Overnight Nut Butter & Honey Oats Serves 2

Overnight Oats (also known as Bircher's Muesli) is the perfect summer alternative to hot porridge oats and a great breakfast on the run as all the work gets done the night before.

1 cup of gluten-free, non-GMO, rolled oats

¼ cup of non-GMO smooth peanut butter or any nut butter

2 tbsp honey

1 tsp pure vanilla extract

Pinch of salt

300 ml almond milk or filtered water

Chopped banana and berries for serving

Add all the ingredients into a deep bowl, mix well and cover with cling film. Pop it in the fridge overnight and serve this creamy delicious oats with banana and berries.

Health benefits

The soluble fibre in **oats** captures bad cholesterol, which makes it one of the most heart-healthy foods you can eat. Oats are a good source of manganese, molybdenum, phosphorus, biotin, magnesium, chromium and zinc (making this a great 'skin food'). **Oats** and **cinnamon** are also beneficial to diabetics as they help stabilise blood sugar levels.

Hemp seeds, very rich in omega-6 and -3 fatty acids, are essentials for heart health and have important anti-inflammatory properties. They are also an excellent source of vitamin E and protein.

Chia seeds are nutritional gold as they are the richest plant-based source of omega-3 fatty acids. Chia seeds are also loaded with protein, antioxidants and minerals.

Walnuts can help reduce bad cholesterol, improve metabolism and aid in weight management. They also possess anti-inflammatory properties and can be a mood booster. Walnuts are also a great source of omega-3 fatty acids.

Gluten & dairy free. Vegan friendly.

Grain-free Granola 8 servings

Serve this granola with live yoghurt and honey, but if you want to avoid dairy altogether, replace the yoghurt with two spoonfuls of tahini and raw honey.

1 tbsp coconut oil, slightly warmed
½ cup of raw almonds
½ cup of raw cashew nuts
Fine pink salt
1 cup of pumpkin seeds
1 cup of raw sunflower seeds
½ cup of sesame seeds
1 cup of desiccated coconut

In a large bowl, stir the coconut oil through the almonds and cashews, adding a pinch of salt. Next place them on a baking sheet and put them in a 150°C preheated oven for 7 minutes, then remove and set aside to cool.

Next, lightly toast the seeds and coconut in a large dry pan for 7 minutes on medium heat, stirring frequently with a wooden spoon, until they become golden in colour. Remove the pan from the heat and allow the seeds and coconut to cool, still giving it a stir now and again while cooling.

Now simply stir all the nuts, seeds and coconut together until it is well mixed and make sure it is properly cooled before storing it in an airtight jar or container.

Health benefits

Nuts and **seeds** are packed with excellent nutrition. Almonds deliver a impressive amount of vitamin E, sesame seeds are high in calcium, cashew nuts are a powerhouse of magnesium and sunflower seeds are also rich in vitamin E and healthy fats. Nuts and seeds are also rich in fibre and protein that will keep hunger at bay for hours.

Gluten, grain & dairy free. Vegan & paleo friendly.

Turmeric Eggs with Spring Onions, Spinach & Tomatoes Serves 2

To kick-start and awaken your metabolism, garnish these eggs with a decent sprinkle of cayenne pepper.

10 cherry tomatoes, halved
2 heaped tsp butter or coconut oil
Pink salt to taste
Pinch of sugar
3 spring onions, finely sliced
1 cup of baby spinach, shredded
1 tsp turmeric
4 organic or free-range eggs, whisked
Lots of freshly cracked black pepper
(optional)

Sauté the cherry tomatoes in 1 teaspoon of butter or coconut oil, a pinch salt and a sprinkling of sugar, to regulate the acidity, for about 4 minutes on high heat and then remove them from the heat.

Sauté the spring onions in the rest of the butter or coconut oil for about 3 minutes, next add the baby spinach and sauté until it's properly wilted.

Lastly, whisk the turmeric and egg together in a separate bowl, and then pour this mixture over the wilted spinach and spring onions, turning the heat up as the eggs are added.

Allow the egg mixture to cook for a minute or so on one side, like you would with an omelette, then with an egg turner carefully turn it over to the other side for another minute or so.

Serve with a drizzle of olive oil, the sautéed cherry tomatoes and freshly ground black pepper.

Health benefits

Eggs are an excellent source of inexpensive complete protein. They are also high in selenium, vitamin D, B12, biotin and minerals like zinc and iron.

Turmeric is a super spice. It contains curcumin which is a powerful anti-inflammatory and antioxidant. Curcumin is best absorbed into the blood stream when eaten with some fat and piperine, which is found in black pepper.

Gluten, grain & dairy free. Paleo friendly.

Mexican Eggs Serves 2

1 small red pepper, diced
1 heaped tbsp butter or coconut oil
1 tsp ground cumin
½ tsp ground coriander
4 organic or free-range eggs, whisked
Pink salt to taste
1 large avocado, peeled & sliced
½ small red onion, finely sliced
¼ cup of fresh coriander leaves, chopped

In a non-stick pan, sauté the diced red pepper until soft. Remove from the pan and set aside.

Heat the butter or coconut oil in a non-stick pan. Whisk in the ground cumin and coriander powders into the eggs and pour the mixture into the hot pan. As the eggs start to cook, season them with salt and turn them over once or twice, you are working towards a soft 'broken omelette' result, not really scrambled. Take the eggs off the heat just before it is cooked through so that they remain soft and delicate.

Serve them plated and topped with the avocado, red onion, sautéed red pepper and coriander leaves.

Health benefits

Eggs are an excellent source of complete protein and are high in selenium, vitamin D, B12, biotin and minerals like zinc and iron. Choline in eggs is essential in healthy skin functioning, and also helps the body maintain proper levels of B vitamins, essential for energy production. Hard-boiled eggs are nature's best packed lunch food, full of nutrients and easy to transport on your daily travels.

Red peppers, also known as capsicums, are very high in vitamin C and A, and are worth including in your diet often. The flavonoids in red peppers are beneficial to preventing cardiovascular disease, and due to the high levels of vitamin A and C in them, they are also effective as an anti-aging food and promote healthy skin.

Red onions are particularly beneficial to diabetics as they help regulate blood sugar levels. Onions also relieve stomach aches and help prevent tooth decay, boost the immune system and can help relieve a sore throat and cough symptoms. They are a good source of minerals such as manganese, potassium and phosphorus, as well as vitamins C and B6, folic acid and thiamine.

Gluten, grain & dairy free. No-carb and paleo friendly.

The Full 'Hippie'   Serves 2

When yearning for a 100% plant-based full 'English' (with lots of protein), then look no further. This can be a no-nonsense, lazy Sunday-morning breakfast if you have some cooked quinoa in the freezer.

1 cup of red or white quinoa

4–6 Portobello mushrooms

Pinch of salt

2 eggs

Sauce:

2 tbsp tahini paste

2 tbsp water

1 tsp garlic salt

To serve:

1 avocado, peeled & quartered

Sprouts of any kind

Olive oil

Micro salad leaves

Start by cooking the quinoa (see pg 72).

Place the mushrooms on a baking tray, season with salt, and pop them in a 170°C preheated oven for 15–20 minutes.

Boil the eggs and while they are cooling, prepare the tahini sauce by simply whisking together the water, tahini and garlic salt.

Peel and halve the eggs, and season them with salt. Assemble the breakfast, plated with a little of everything and a drizzle of olive oil.

Health benefits

Quinoa is a complete protein with a cup of it containing about 8 grams of protein; it has twice as much fibre as most grains and is also rich in manganese, magnesium, phosphorus, zinc, iron and copper.

Portobello mushrooms are a good source of plant protein with lots of fibre, and are low in carbohydrates, making them a great addition to a weight-loss eating plan. Portobello mushrooms are also high in phosphorus, B vitamins, copper and selenium.

Avocados are truly a superfood. Their health benefits are endless, but to just name a few: they are rich in potassium, folic acid, vitamin E, B vitamins and fibre. They also play an important role in assisting your body to absorb phytonutrients and antioxidants.

Gluten, grain & dairy free. Paleo friendly.

Shakshuka Serves 2

This breakfast will be a revelation; easy to prepare, delicious, filling and carb-free.

1 large onion, diced

1 large red pepper, diced

1 tbsp coconut oil

3 cloves of garlic, freshly crushed

1 tsp ground cumin

1 tsp sweet paprika

300 ml jar of plain tomato passata, or a
    400 g tin of chopped tomatoes

½ tsp sugar

1 tsp pink salt

4 eggs

⅓ cup of fresh coriander leaves, chopped

Fry the onion and chopped pepper in coconut oil until soft, and then add the crushed garlic and spices and fry for a further 2 minutes. Add the pasata or chopped tomatoes, sugar and salt, and let it all simmer together for 10 minutes on medium heat.

Now transfer the spiced tomato sauce to a fairly deep baking dish, and then break the eggs into the sauce, taking care not to break the yolks. Place the dish in a 180°C preheated oven and bake for 10 minutes. Remove the dish from the oven, and sprinkle the eggs with black pepper and chopped coriander before serving.

Health benefits

Eggs are an excellent source of inexpensive complete protein. They are also high in selenium, vitamin D, B12, biotin and minerals like zinc and iron.

Tomatoes are rich in vitamin C and A, both of which fight infections and are essential for immune health. Tomatoes are also famously high in lycopene that protects our skin from ultraviolet damage and oxidative stress, as well as reducing the risk of osteoporosis. Try and include cooked tomatoes in your diet frequently as their lycopene content increases with cooking.

Gluten, grain & dairy free. Paleo friendly.

Sakkie's Sourdough Serves 2

My friend Sakkie is a farmer who has a passion for baking bread using traditional methods. Sakkie has learnt to acquire patience and mindfulness as sourdough takes time and every loaf requires love and attention and can become a very rewarding and therapeutic process.

The art of combining flour and water to make a sourdough starter has been practised by bakers for thousands of years. When you combine water with flour and leave it to ferment, this turns into a starter, or what is sometimes called the 'mother'. This starter is then used instead of instant yeast to act as a raising agent.

How to create your sourdough starter

Day 1: Mix 1 cup of flour with ½ a cup of water and place this mixture in a large jar.

Days 2, 3, 4, 5: On each of these days, take out and discard most of the flour mixture and add 1 cup of flour with ½ cup of water and mix it in well. This process is called 'feeding' the sourdough starter to keep it strong and 'alive'. As the days pass, more and more bubbles will begin to form in the jar, and this is your 'starter' for your bread.

After day 5, place 3 tablespoons of the starter into a large bowl, and mix into it 1 generous cup of bread flour and ⅔ of a cup of lukewarm water, mixing it well. It should have the consistency of thick porridge. Now cover the bowl and allow it to ferment at room temperature overnight. The next morning drop a spoonful of the above mixture into a glass of water, if it floats up to the top then this mixture is ready; if not, it is best to start over.

1⅓ cups lukewarm water (25–30°C)
⅔ cup sourdough starter
3 cups unbleached white bread flour
⅓ cup brown bread flour
1 tsp salt

To a large mixing bowl, add the lukewarm water, the sourdough starter, the bread flours and salt. Mix together with a wooden spoon, or with your hands if necessary, until it comes together as a dough. Use a spatula to ensure all the dry bits on the side get mixed in as well.

Cover the bowl and let it rest for 40 minutes.

Next turn the dough out on a work surface dusted generously with 'white' unbleached flour. Now stretch and fold the dough into a roughly shaped ball, then return it to the bowl and allow it to rest under a tea towel for 40 minutes.

Repeat the kneading and resting process twice again. When folding and stretching is completed for the third time, transfer it to a well-floured container and allow it to rise for 3–4 hours.

30 minutes before baking, preheat the oven to 240°C.

When the dough has doubled in volume, turn it out onto a non-stick baking sheet, shape it and then scour the top of the dough carefully to create pretty ridges on the finished bread.

Bake the dough for 24 minutes. Remove the loaf from the oven now, and roll it into a tea towel, allowing it to cool down for at least 30 minutes before serving. This 30 minutes is an ongoing baking period for the bread.

Tip: Using a spray bottle filled with water, spray a mist into the oven after 5 minutes of baking to expand the dough even more before the crust is formed. As sourdough baking is a slow, time-consuming process, it is perhaps worth doubling the amounts of ingredients to make two loaves, one of which can be frozen when it has cooled down properly.

Health benefits of a sourdough starter

Not only does this fermented starter give the bread a delicious taste, it has many health benefits, for example:

– The sourdough starter does not cause bloating and discomfort when eaten, unlike instant yeast that causes havoc with our digestive system.

– Using a sourdough starter as your raising agent helps the gluten content in the bread to diminish drastically. Often those with gluten sensitivities find that their bodies are compatible with true sourdough.

NB: To ensure that your sourdough is even more nutritious you should choose an unbleached, stone-ground, non-GMO flour. Stone-milled, unbleached flour still contains all of the wheat's nutritional value as bleaching and heat-process milling destroys nutrients.

Sourdough Toast & Toppings Serves 2

Here are three simple topping variations of sublime sourdough toast. The perfect breakfast for a lazy Saturday morning.

Avocado & Tomato

Avocado
Pink salt
Olive oil
Tomato
Freshly ground pepper

Mash the avocado with some salt and olive oil, then spread a generous layer of it onto the toast. Top with thinly sliced tomatoes and season with some freshly ground pepper and a sprinkling of pink salt.

Honey, Banana & Nut Butter Dream

Cashew & almond butter
Honey
Sliced banana

Start by smothering the toast with some nut butter, then a layer of honey, and lastly the banana, thinly sliced into coins.

White Beans & Pesto

Tinned cannellini (white) beans
Pesto (see page 34)

Drain the beans well and mash them with a fork. Layer the toast with the mashed beans and then a drizzle of pesto.

Health benefits of sourdough bread

Generally, one should avoid eating bread more than once every couple of days, especially the ordinary store-bought, massed-produced, GMO, preservative-rich kind. But I make a happy exception for true **sourdough**, made from stone ground, unbleached non-GMO flour bread and here is why:

Stone ground, unbleached flour retains all its excellent health benefits and nutrition that wheat has to offer (there is a good reason why bread has been a staple food for hundreds of years), and when the bread is made from the true sourdough method it actually helps breakdown the gluten in the wheat and makes it much easier to digest.

So unless you have celiac disease, there is no reason why a few delicious sourdough slices shouldn't be enjoyed every now and again.

True sourdough is mostly available from good bakeries and farmers' markets.

Dairy free. Vegan friendly.

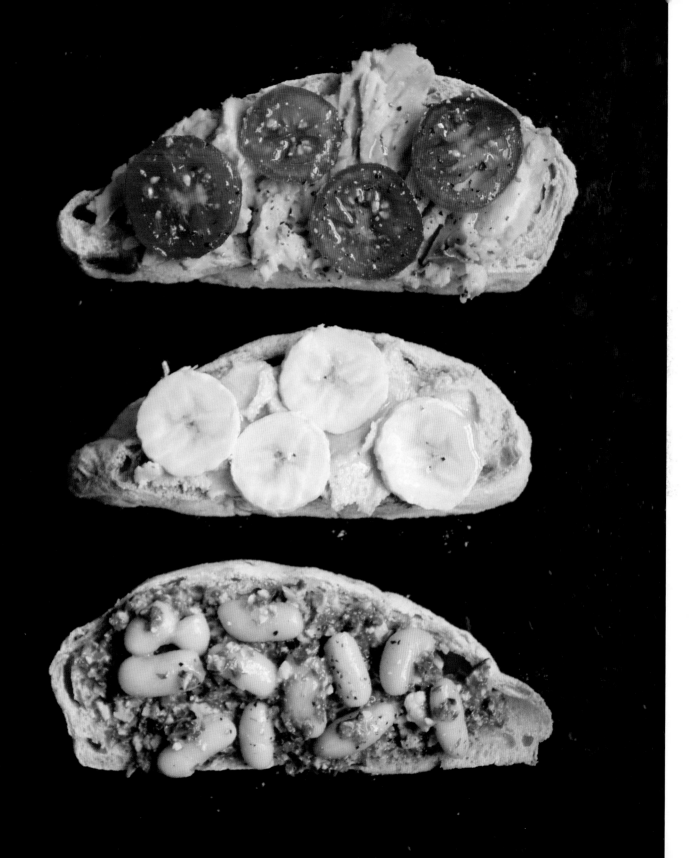

Raw

Nut & Seed Butters

These nut & seed butters are great toppings for sourdough toast with honey & banana (see page 22), delicious with salads and a wonderful alternative to yoghurt with my grain-free granola (see page 10).

Making nut butters does require a little patience and persistence as the nuts will first become crumbly, then after a while powdery, but just keep going because eventually the nuts will start releasing their oils and then it becomes a firm paste and finally this dreamy creamy paste emerges that makes you want to eat it straight out of the jar. It could take up to 30 minutes of processing with breaks to become a nut butter, so don't give up.

Do not add any water or oil to the nuts as they process, just be patient and remember to give your food processor well deserved breaks!

Cashew & Almond Butter Yields 1 cup

1 cup of raw cashews
1 cup of raw almonds
Pinch of salt

Place all the nuts on a baking tray to lightly roast for 7–10 minutes in a 150°C preheated oven, then remove and cool them for a minute or two.

Now transfer the nuts and salt to your food processor and start pulsing for a minute at a time. (It is important to give the food processor's motor a break, otherwise it may burn out.)

Store your nut butter in a tightly sealed jar at room temperature in a dark cupboard. It should keep for about 10 days.

Nut & Seed Butter Yields 1 cup

1 cup of raw cashews
½ cup of raw sunflower seeds
½ cup of raw pumpkin seeds
½ teaspoon of fine pink salt

Toast the sunflower seeds and pumpkin seeds for approximately 7 minutes in a dry skillet, stirring frequently with a wooden spoon to ensure that all sides are toasted equally.

Place the nuts on a baking tray and toast them for 10 minutes in a 150°C preheated oven. Remove them and allow a minute or two to cool.

Now transfer the nuts and seeds, as well as the salt to your food processor and start pulsing for a minute at a time. (It is important to give the food processor's motor a break.)

Store your nut butter in a tightly sealed jar at room temperature in a dark cupboard. It should keep well for about 10 days.

(continued on following page)

(Nut and Seed Butters Continued)

Homemade Tahini Paste Yields ½ cup

I use tahini in salad dressings, sauces and on homemade granola. Homemade tahini often has a far superior taste to the store-bought versions, which can often acquire a bitter taste when not as fresh as they should be.

1 cup of hulled sesame seeds
½ teaspoon of pink salt
2 tbsp mild-flavoured olive oil

Toast the sesame seeds for approximately 5 minutes in a dry skillet on medium heat, stirring frequently with a wooden spoon to ensure that all sides are toasted equally to a light golden colour.

Now transfer the seeds, as well as the salt and oil to your food processor and start pulsing for a minute at a time. Keep going at 1-minute intervals until you have smooth, creamy consistency.

Store the tahini in the refrigerator in a well-sealed jar, and it will keep for approximately 30 days.

Health benefits

Almonds are rich in vitamin E, omega-3 fatty acids, protein, manganese, zinc and calcium. I recommend soaking almonds overnight before use as this deactivates the enzyme-inhibiting compound found in their skin.

Cashews are high in magnesium, a mineral which most people are deficient in due to large-scale farming. Magnesium is involved in over 200 functions in our bodies. Cashews also contain vitamin E, copper, iron and selenium.

Sesame seeds are excellent for promoting bone health due to their impressive calcium, zinc and phosphorus content. Sesame seeds are also rich in magnesium and copper and additionally contain excellent anti-inflammatory properties.

Sunflower seeds are very rich in vitamin E, contain good quantities of B vitamins, selenium and copper and essential fatty acids (healthy fats) that are the building blocks for cell membranes, and in balancing hormones and reducing inflammation.

Nut butters are gluten, grain & dairy free and are both vegan & paleo friendly.

Sprouting Yields 1–2 cups

The most important tip for successful sprouting is to select and use non-GMO seeds, beans or pulses.

2 tbsp mung beans
3 tbsp alfalfa seeds
2 tbsp whole lentils

Only choose one of the above per jar.

What you need:
1 large, sterilised, wide-mouth mason/
  preserving jar
1 square of muslin cloth or fine mesh
1 elastic band

Start by sterilising your jar.

Next add the seeds, beans or lentils to the jar, then cover the top with the muslin and secure it with an elastic band; this allows for water to be added and drained through the cloth or mesh. Rinse the beans, legumes or seeds well with fresh water, at least 3–4 times to get rid of impurities.

Once the repeated rinsing has been done, add filtered water to the beans, seeds, or lentils (add enough water to immerse and cover them with about 2cm of water above the surface of the beans, seeds or lentils. Leave them to soak for about 12 hours overnight.

The next morning drain away the excess water, rinse them again and then once more drain them well (all excess water should be drained), then leave the jar, covered with the muslin cloth or mesh secured with the elastic band at room temperature in a cool dark area.

For the next 2–3 days you should rinse and drain the sprouts well every 12 hours, returning them to the dark storing area every time.

Use the sprouts within the next 5 days, storing them in the fridge in an airtight container.

Health benefits

Sprouted mung beans have impressive amounts of protein and are very rich in vitamin C and K, as well as manganese and copper. Sprouts have the ability to improve digestion, boost metabolism, increase enzymatic activity and lower cholesterol. Sprouts should be eaten raw as they lose the nutrients rapidly when heated.

Alfalfa sprouts are a good source of calcium, vitamins K and C.

Sprouted lentils are high in amino acids; methionine and cysteine are two amino acids important for muscle building and strengthening of our body.

Dressings & Sauces

Any salad or healthy dish can be made delicious and even more nutritious with the right dressing or sauce. The recipes that follow are all gluten, grain and dairy free as well as vegan and paleo friendly.

Coriander Vegan Pesto Yields 150 ml or ⅔ cup

This pesto goes especially well with the Green Goddess Salad (see page 58) and the Black Bean Salad Leaf Boats (see page 67).

2 cups of loosely packed, fresh, washed and
   spin-dried coriander leaves
125 ml olive oil
Juice of ½ a lemon
½ cup of cashew nuts
1 clove of garlic, crushed
Pink salt to taste

Add all the ingredients to your food processor, and pulse until you have a course pesto consistency.

Creamy Cashew Dressing Yields ⅓ cup

This dressing is a great vegan alternative to a Caeser dressing and works especially well with the Roasted Chickpea Salad (see page 56).

½ cup of raw cashew nuts, soaked in water
   for at least 30 minutes
1 tsp of garlic salt
Juice of one small lemon, or half a large
   lemon
1 tbsp tahini paste
2 tbsp olive oil
50 ml water

Drain the soaked cashew nuts and add them along with all the remaining ingredients to your blender jug and pulse until you have a smooth mixture.

Harissa Paste Yields ½ cup

Use this paste to add to salads, stews, soup or to dress Dressed Up Mushrooms (see page 92).

3 sundried tomatoes

4 dried red chillies (any variety will do)

1 tsp caraway seeds

1 tsp coriander seeds

1 tsp cumin seeds

½ tsp paprika

3 cloves of garlic, peeled

1 tsp pink salt

4 tbsp cold-pressed olive oil

Juice of ½ a lemon

Place the sundried tomatoes and chillies in a heat-proof bowl, cover them with boiling water and let them soak for 30 minutes

Toast the whole spices in a dry pan or skillet over low–medium heat, stirring them occasionally. When the spices become fragrant remove from the heat and transfer them to a bowl to cool. Once cooled grind them into a fine texture with a coffee grinder or mortar and pestle.

Drain the tomatoes and chillies. Next stem and de-seed the chillies, and then combine all the ingredients in your food processor and pulse until you have a smooth consistency (scrape down the sides if necessary). Store it in an airtight jar in the fridge, adding a thin layer of olive oil over the top before securing the lid onto the jar.

Spicy Peanut Sauce Yields 1 cup

This sauce goes especially well with Summer Rolls (see page 66) and Chicken Skewers (see page 136).

50 ml peanut butter

1 small 200g tin of coconut milk

1 tbsp Thai red curry paste

1 tsp white wine vinegar

1 tsp sugar

2 tbsp water

Pink salt to taste

Add all the ingredients to your blender jug, and pulse until you have smooth mixture.

(continued on following page)

Turmeric & Tahini Dressing Yields ⅓ cup

I love using turmeric for its amazing health benefits and this sauce works well to liven up brown rice, beans or quinoa or added to a Yoga Kitchen Bowl (see page 64). Store any leftover sauce in the fridge where it should keep well for 3–4 days.

1 tsp turmeric powder
½ tsp garam masala
2 tbsp tahini paste
1 tbsp olive oil
1 clove of garlic, crushed
50 ml water
Pink salt to taste

Add all the ingredients to a jar, then secure the lid tightly and shake until it is a smooth mixture.

Homemade 'Ketchup' Yields ¼ cup

This simple sauce delivers on taste and health benefits. Use it to dress a bowl of quinoa served with raw shredded veggies like carrots, spring onion and spinach.

3 tsp tomato puree
1 tsp brown sugar
2 tbsp olive oil
1 tbsp fresh lemon juice
Pinch of cayenne pepper (omit for children)
Pink salt to taste

Use a jar to combine all the ingredients and then screw the lid on to the jar securely and shake until it is a smooth mixture.

Sweet & Sour Sauce Yields a little more than 1 cup

¼ cup of honey
¼ cup of white wine vinegar
½ cup of tomato sauce/ketchup
¼ cup of pineapple, chopped finely
1 tsp soy sauce
2 spring onions, finely sliced

Combine all the ingredients, except the spring onions, in a sauce pan, and let it simmer for 5 minutes on medium heat. When cool, stir through the spring onions.

Mango Chutney Yields 1 cup

2 large ripe mangoes, peeled and sliced
1 tsp pink salt
2 cloves of garlic, crushed
1 cup of golden castor sugar
½ tbsp English mustard powder
1 tbsp ginger, finely grated
¾ cup of white wine vinegar
1 tsp cayenne pepper

Place the mango slices in a bowl and sprinkle them with salt, and store in the fridge overnight; in the morning drain the juice.

Add the garlic, sugar, mustard, ginger, vinegar and cayenne pepper in a sauce pan and stir over a low heat until all the sugar is dissolved. Then add the mango slices and bring it to the boil, simmering for 30 minutes until the chutney is thick and syrupy.

Spoon into a sterilised preserving jar and seal. Store in fridge once opened.

Homemade Hummus Yields 1 cup

1 tin of chickpeas (reserve some of the liquid), or ½ cup of dry chickpeas, cooked and drained (see page 56)
Juice of 1 small lemon
1 clove of fresh garlic, crushed
2 tbsp of tahini paste (see page 30)
30 ml of cold-pressed olive oil
1 tsp cayenne pepper (optional)
½ tsp pink salt

In a blender add all the ingredients together with about ¼ of the chickpea tin liquid or 50 ml of the cooking water. Blend until you have a smooth consistency.

Health benefits

All sauces are gluten, grain & dairy free.

Probiotic-rich Cultured Vegetables

Cultured or fermented vegetables are a wonderful and tasty way to get all the probiotics (good bacteria) that your body needs. To avoid adding harmful pesticides to your ferments, it is important to use organic vegetables where possible as the skin of the vegetables are mostly left on. More importantly, organic vegetables will have more lactobacilli present, which will make for a much better ferment. Probiotics are hugely important for good digestion and a strong immune system.

To sterilise your fermenting jar, wash it in warm soapy water, then rinse it well and next simply dunk it in a large saucepan with boiling water.

Use clean, filtered water for making the brine; unfiltered tap water should be boiled and cooled before making a brine with it. The ratio of 3 tablespoons of salt to 1 litre of water is a good combination to make brine for fermenting.

Kimchi

Fills one 300 ml preserving jar

1 small savoy cabbage or napa cabbage

¼ cup of sea salt

Filtered water

2 cloves of garlic, finely grated

1 small (thumb-size) knob of ginger, finely grated

1 tsp sugar

2 tbsp fish sauce or water

1 tbsp water

1 tsp red pepper or chilli flakes

6 spring onions, trimmed and finely sliced

silicone/surgical gloves (optional)

sterilised preserving jar

Remove the core from the cabbage and then slice it in 2.5 cm-wide ribbons, lengthways. Add the cabbage and salt to a large bowl, start massaging (wearing the gloves) the salt into the cabbage until the cabbage releases some fluid and begins to soften. Next, add enough water to cover the top layer of the cabbage and put a plate with something heavy to weigh it down on top, like a jar of preserves. Leave it to stand this way for an hour. After an hour has passed, rinse the cabbage under cold water twice, then let it drain in a colander.

Start making the paste by mixing the garlic, ginger, fish sauce, water, sugar and red pepper flakes together in a bowl to form a paste.

Gently squeeze and press any remaining water from the cabbage and then return it to your large bowl along with the spring onions and paste. Using your hands (and this is where the gloves come in handy), gently work the paste into the cabbage and onions thoroughly.

Once the cabbage is coated evenly, transfer it to a preserving jar, packing it tightly and pressing down onto the top surface when the jar is filled so that the saucy brine covers the surface of the cabbage. Also be sure to leave at least 2 cm of 'headspace' above the surface of the brine/sauce.

Then seal the jar well with its lid and store the fermenting kimchi at room temperature for 2–5 days. You should open the jar once a day to let it release its gases and to press down on the cabbage to ensure it is still submerged under the brine/sauce. Be warned: Kimchi can be smelly while fermenting with a typically strong smell due to the garlic, fish sauce and onions. After 2 days (in summer) or 4–5 days (in winter) of room temperature fermenting, transfer the jar to the fridge and start enjoying this wildly delicious condiment with meals.

Kvass Fills one litre jar

4–6 medium, organic beetroot
1½ tbsp sea salt
Filtered water, boiled
1 large preserving jar

Scrub the beetroot thoroughly and then top, tail and quarter them, leaving their skin on, and then pack them into the sterilised jar. Dissolve the salt properly in boiled water and add it to the jar. The brine should cover the surface of the beetroot pieces.

Seal the jar well with its lid and store the fermenting beetroot at room temperature for 2–5 days. You should open the jar once a day to let it release its gases and to press down on the beetroot to ensure they are still submerged under the brine. After 2 days (in summer) and 4–5 days (in winter) of room temperature fermenting, transfer the jar to the fridge and start enjoying the fermented beetroot with meals. The beetroot will acquire a tart, pickled taste.

Za'atar Salad Serves 4–6

1 large aubergine, chopped into
   1-inch cubes

Salt

Coconut oil

1 cup of cooked quinoa (red or white)

½ cup of baby plum tomatoes, chopped

1 red pepper, diced

¼ cup of mint leaves, chopped (optional)

¼ cup of flat leaf parsley, chopped

½ a red onion, chopped

Juice of ½ a lemon

2 tsp ground cumin

½ tsp ground sumac

1 tbsp dried thyme

1 tsp pink salt

4 tbsp cold-pressed olive oil

½ cup of hulled white sesame seeds,
   lightly toasted

Season the aubergine with salt, and place on a tray greased with coconut oil. Then roast in a 180°C preheated oven for approximately 20 minutes.

While the aubergine is roasting, cook the quinoa (see page 72).

Assemble the salad by adding the cooled aubergine and quinoa together with the tomatoes, peppers, fresh herbs, salt, oil, dried ground spices and thyme to a large bowl and gently mix them all together, sprinkling over the toasted sesame seeds just before serving.

Health benefits

Aubergines, also known as eggplant or brinjal, have an impressive spectrum of nutrients, fibre, folic acid, potassium, manganese, as well as vitamins C, K and B6, phosphorous, copper, thiamine, niacin, magnesium and pantothenic acid. The phytonutrient nasunin in the skin of the aubergine is a powerful anti-oxidant that protects brain cells against free radical damage.

Tomatoes also have a wide variety of healthful nutrients like vitamins A, C (to fight infections) and K, potassium (controlling heart rate and blood pressure), manganese and vitamin E, thiamine, niacin, vitamin B6 and folic acid, magnesium and phosphorus.

Quinoa is an excellent source of complete protein and fibre.

Gluten, grain & dairy free. Vegan & paleo friendly.

Rainbow Slaw Serves 4–6

½ cup of red cabbage, shredded

½ cup of white cabbage, shredded

½ cup carrot, grated

¾ cup of cooked red quinoa

½ red onion, finely sliced

50 ml toasted sesame oil

2 tbsp raw apple cider vinegar

1 tbsp honey

1 clove of garlic, crushed

½ tsp pink salt

1 avocado, diced or sliced

3 tbsp white sesame seeds, lightly toasted

(For a bit of creaminess why not add a
tablespoon of tahini)

Combine all the shredded and grated vegetables in a large bowl, then simply add the cooked, cooled quinoa, all the dressing ingredients and then toss. Lastly, sprinkle with the toasted sesame seeds and plate the slaw with the avocado.

Health benefits

Red & white cabbage contain a wide variety of vitamins and minerals in significant amounts, but apart from that the phytonutrients in cabbage with their amazing health benefits makes it, in my opinion, an affordable superfood that should be included in your diet at least 3 times a week.

The phytonutrients in cabbage can assist in detoxification, blood cleansing, eye strengthening, and can help to heal stomach ulcers and treat fungus infections. They also fight lung and colon cancer.

Cabbage is also very high in sulforaphane, which stimulates the production of glutathione, which is the most important, internally produced antioxidant to play an important role in liver detoxification.

The vitamin C content in red cabbage is 6–8 times higher than green cabbage. Cabbage eaten raw, or lightly steamed, is far more beneficial than when well-cooked.

Gluten, grain & dairy free. Vegan & paleo friendly.

Asian 'Crunch' Salad Serves 4-6

1 cup of cooked corn on the cob or thawed
and blanched frozen corn

2 baby savoy cabbages, finely shredded

2 carrots, shredded

1 cup of mixed sprouts

2 sprigs of spring onions

Dressing:

30 ml toasted sesame oil

1 clove of garlic

Juice of 1 medium lemon

1 tbsp raw honey

Pink salt to taste

1/3 cup of roasted cashew nuts (optional)

Simply mix the corn and shredded vegetables in a large salad bowl. Put all the dressing ingredients in a glass jar and mix well, or whisk them together in a bowl. Dress the salad. Lastly, sprinkle the roasted cashews and serve.

Health benefits

Savoy cabbage is very high in vitamin C, boosting the immune system, acting as a powerful antioxidant and promoting collagen production. Cabbage also provides a huge amount of fibre and other vitamins and minerals along with sulphur which helps fight infection and assists in wound healing. Cabbage is best eaten raw, lightly stir-fried or steamed.

Sweet corn is packed with beneficial fibre, is rich in vitamin A and significant B vitamin levels. Sweet corn is also rich in a whole host of phytonutrients, which promote healthy vision, mucusa and skin, helps reduce inflammation and fight certain types of cancers. Furthermore sweet corn also contains important minerals like zinc, copper, magnesium, iron and manganese.

Sprouts have an impressive list of health benefits. Seeds, grains and beans can be sprouted, which increases their nutrient and enzyme content to promote good digestion and kick start metabolic acid. The importance of digestive enzymes are often overlooked and missing from our diets. See my sprout tutorial on page 32 to start sprouting at home; it is an affordable and simple way to give your health a huge boost.

Gluten & dairy free. Vegan friendly.

Butternut & Kale 'Chip' Salad Serves 4–6

For those who are wary of kale, this is the way to eat it: the crunchy, nutty taste of kale chips are so amazing that even those most opposed to greens cannot resist them. This salad is perfect for winter and works particularly well served alongside a comforting soup.

Tip: Soak the almonds the night before, then drain them the next morning and let them dry on a paper towel before roasting them. (See lifestyle tips & tools on page xii for more information on the benefits of soaking nuts and legumes.)

1 medium-sized whole butternut

Coconut oil

12 large leaves of kale, de-stemmed

Pinch of pink salt or a dash of soy sauce

¼ cup of raw almonds

¼ cup of raw pumpkin seeds

Dressing:

30 ml olive oil

Juice of ½ a lemon

½ tsp ground cumin

Pinch of paprika

Pinch of cayenne pepper

Wash the butternut thoroughly. Leaving the skin on, remove the stalk and then slice the butternut lengthways into 2-cm-thick wedges. Place them on an oven-proof dish greased with coconut oil and transfer it to a 180°C preheated oven. Remove the butternut after 30 minutes and leave to cool.

Turn the oven temperature down to 120°C and place the washed and thoroughly dried kale leaves flat on a greased baking tray (you may need to use more than one tray to accommodate all the leaves). Season with a sprinkle of pink salt or dash of soy sauce. Then transfer them to the oven for approximately 20 minutes. They should be crispy and flaky when they are done.

While the kale is roasting, toast the almonds and pumpkin seeds in a dry pan, stirring frequently and watching them closely. When they start swelling they are ready and can be set aside to cool.

Assemble the kale chips, butternut wedges, nuts and seeds on a platter or shallow salad bowl. Whisk all the dressing ingredients together and drizzle over the salad before serving.

Health benefits

Kale can legitimately be labelled as a superfood; it is extremely high in vitamins A, C and K and is crammed full of phytonutrients that aid in DNA cell repair, slow down cancer cell growth, particularly those that protect against colon and prostrate cancer. The list of health benefits of kale is long and there are simply too many to mention, but let me end with a fun fact: kale is super easy to grow, and so why not try to grow and harvest your very own organic kale to add to salads, soups, stews or to make kale chips from.

Gluten, grain & dairy free. Vegan & paleo friendly.

Salad No-Çoise Serves 2

This vegetarian version of a Salad Niçoise is easy and fast to prepare. Although it's not 100% plant-based I am huge fan of eggs as they deliver on protein and nutrition in a no-fuss manner.

4 large eggs

Handful of French (fine) green beans

2 baby gem lettuces

1 large avocado

2 tbsp capers, chopped

½ a red onion, finely sliced

1/3 cup of Kalamata olives, de-pipped

Dressing:

20 ml white wine vinegar

40 ml olive oil

1 tsp sugar

Black pepper to taste

Pink salt to taste

Boil the eggs for 7 minutes and then drain away the water and allow them to cool.

Next top and tail the green beans and then blanch them in boiling water for about 3 minutes. Drain them well and season lightly with salt.

Now prep the gem lettuce by removing the stems, separating and washing the leaves and spinning them dry in a salad spinner. Peel and quarter the avocado and then you are ready to start on the salad dressing: add all the dressing ingredients to a small jar, screw the lid on securely and shake until it has formed a smooth emulsion.

Now assemble your salad, adding the lettuce, peeled and halved eggs, green beans, avocado, onions, olives and capers to a shallow bowl or plate. Dress and serve.

Health benefits

Olives are often overlooked for their health benefits in comparison to olive oil (which should by the way only be consumed when it has been cold pressed). Whole preserved olives have an astounding array of antioxidant and anti-inflammatory properties. They are also rich in good fats and worth choosing over other snacks for precisely these reasons.

Eggs are an excellent source of inexpensive complete protein. They are also high in selenium, vitamins D and B12, biotin and minerals like zinc and iron.

Green beans are rich in a wide variety of vitamins and minerals as well as omega-3 fatty acids and many different phytonutrients that have all been shown to have heart-health-supportive antioxidant properties. Their fibre content is also impressive and since they are so tasty and easy to prepare, they are a great addition to your diet on a regular basis: add them to stews, salads and Thai curries.

Gluten, grain & dairy free. Paleo friendly.

Daily Detox Salad
Serves 4–6 as side-salad portions

This salad is quick and simple to prepare, and contains a huge amount of health benefits. I often serve it as a side salad with a protein dish at supper, or simply alongside a humble baked potato for lunch.

1 baby red cabbage
2 medium carrots, grated
½ cup of kale or spinach, sliced finely

Dressing:
25 ml raw apple cider vinegar
50 ml cold-pressed olive oil
1 tbsp raw honey
1 clove of garlic, freshly crushed or grated
Pinch of pink salt

Remove the outer layers and core of the cabbage and then slice it as finely as possible. Simply combine all the prepped vegetables in a large bowl and toss. Then combine all the dressing ingredients in a jar, screw the lid on securely and shake well. Dress and serve.

Health benefits

Red cabbage contains a wide variety of vitamins and minerals in significant amounts, but the phytonutrients in it with their amazing health benefits makes cabbage, in my opinion, an affordable superfood that should be included in your diet at least 3 times a week.

The phytonutrients in cabbage can assist in detoxification, blood cleansing, and eye strengthening, and can help to heal stomach ulcers and treat fungus infections. Cabbage can also fight lung and colon cancer.

Cabbage is also very high in sulforaphane, which stimulates the production of glutathione, which is the most important internally produced antioxidant and plays an important role in liver detoxification.

Carrots are very high in vitamin A, essential for vision and healthy skin and an important protector against infection; vitamin C, essential for immune health and collagen production; vitamins K and B8, panthogenic acid, folic acid (folate), potassium, iron, copper and manganese.

Raw apple cider vinegar is rich in enzymes and potassium, and can assist in digestion and in the maintenance of a healthy body pH balance.

Gluten, grain & dairy free. Vegan & paleo friendly.

Roasted Chickpea Salad Serves 4–6

1 cup of dried chickpeas, soaked overnight or two tins of chickpeas (make sure it comes in a BPA-free tin)

½ tsp sweet paprika

½ tsp ground cumin

1 head of cos lettuce, de-stemmed and washed

6 large kale leaves, de-stemmed and finely sliced

½ cup of hulled white sesame seeds

½ tsp garlic salt

2 tbsp olive oil

Pink salt to taste

Creamy Cashew Dressing (see page 34)

Follow the package instructions when soaking and cooking the chickpeas from dry. Once cooked, drain well and allow them to cool. Transfer them to greased baking trays and spread them in a single layer. Season with salt and lightly dust them with sweet paprika and ground cumin. Place the trays in a 180°C preheated oven and allow them to roast for 15–20 minutes, removing the tray once or twice during roasting, to give it a good shake ensuring evenly roasted chickpeas.

Transfer the greens to a large bowl.

Toast the seeds lightly in a dry pan and set them aside to cool. Once cooled transfer them to your food processor, adding the olive oil and garlic salt, and pulse, or grind them with a mortar and pestle, until you have a crushed consistency.

When the chickpeas are ready remove them from the oven and allow a few minutes to cool, then add them to the greens and dress with the cashew dressing. Lastly, sprinkle over the crushed sesame seeds and serve.

Health benefits

Chickpeas are an excellent source of manganese, magnesium, copper, zinc, and vitamins B1 and B6. They are also rich in dietary fibre and polyunsaturated fatty acids, and a great source of plant protein and phytonutrients like quercetin and kaempferol (which alleviates bruising oedema, varicose veins, etc.). Phytonutrients protect our bodies against free radical damage and infections that could lead to cancer.

Kale can legitimately be labelled as a superfood. It is extremely high in vitamins A, C and K and is crammed full of phytonutrients that aid in DNA cell repair, slow down cancer cell growth and others that particularly protect against colon and prostrate cancer.

Gluten, grain & dairy free. Vegan friendly.

Green Goddess Salad Serves 4–6

8 Brussels sprouts, halved

2 large courgettes, sliced into 1-cm-thick slices

Salt to season vegetables

Coconut oil

10 spears of tender-stem broccoli

10 fine spears of asparagus, woody stems removed

½ cup of pumpkin seeds, lightly toasted

2 medium avocados

2 cups of loosely packed watercress salad leaves

Coriander Pesto (see page 34)

Preheat the oven to 170°C. On a large baking tray lay out the Brussels sprouts and sliced courgettes evenly, season with salt and add a knob of coconut oil to grease the pan. Place it in oven to roast the vegetables for 30 minutes, removing and shaking the pan after a few minutes to ensure all the vegetables are covered in a bit of oil.

Blanch, or flash-boil for 1 minute, the broccoli and asparagus and then drain and season with salt.

Toast the pumpkin seeds in a dry pan on medium heat for approximately 7 minutes, stirring frequently, then remove them from the heat and allow them to cool.

Peel and quarter the avocados. Place the pumpkin seeds in the oven for the last 3 minutes of the Brussels sprout/courgettes roasting time.

Remove the roasted vegetables and allow all to cool for a few minutes, and then assemble in a large, shallow bowl: a layer of watercress leaves, next blanched veggies, then roasted veggies, and lastly the avocado and pumpkin seeds. Dress with dollops of pesto and serve.

Health benefits

Asparagus is rich in vitamins A, C and E. It also has potent anti-inflammatory and antioxidant properties that fight cancer and diabetes and is important for maintaining heart health. Asparagus is also a powerful digestive aid as it contains high amounts of the nutrient inulin, which acts as a prebiotic (food for good bacteria). An excellent source of fibre, it contains a surprising amount of plant-based protein.

Brussels sprouts are exceptionally healthy as part of the cruciferous vegetable family that contain powerful cancer-fighting glucosinolates. Brussels sprouts top them all when it comes to total content.

Broccoli, especially the tender-stem variety, is a powerhouse of nutrition containing large amounts of vitamins and minerals, glucosinolates, flavanoids and a wide variety of other antioxidant compounds.

Gluten, grain & dairy free. Vegan & paleo friendly.

Nachos Salad   Serves 4–6

Kids love this 'chippie' salad and one must lunge at every imaginable opportunity to get a few veggies into them!

Salt to taste
1 clove of garlic, crushed
Juice of half a lime, or small lemon
Dash of olive oil
2 avocados, mashed
1 cup of lightly salted, non-GMO corn
  chips
1 cup of frozen sweet corn, blanched and
  drained well

Salsa:
1 cup of cherry tomatoes, quartered
4 spring onions, finely sliced
1 green chilli, deseeded and finely
  chopped
¼ cup of fresh coriander leaves, chopped
50 ml olive oil
Pink salt to taste
½ tsp brown sugar

Prep the salsa first by chopping the tomatoes, spring onions, chilli and coriander, adding them all into a bowl. Then add the olive oil, salt and a sprinkle of brown sugar, and then mix all together well, and place in the fridge for 15 minutes for the flavours to infuse.

Add a pinch of salt, the crushed garlic, the lime/ lemon juice and the olive oil to the mashed avocados, mixing it through gently.

Using a shallow salad bowl, lay out the corn chips, add a dollop of mashed avocado here and there, sprinkle over the corn, and lastly add a scoop of salsa here and there, and serve.

Health benefits

Sweet corn is packed with beneficial fibre, is rich in vitamin A and significant B vitamin levels. It is also rich in a whole host of phytonutrients, which promote healthy vision, mucusa and skin, help reduce inflammation and fight certain types of cancers. Furthermore sweet corn also contains important minerals like zinc, copper, magnesium, iron and manganese.

Avocados are abundant in healthy fats and fibre and will give you sustained energy throughout the day. Avocados are also rich in vitamin E and folic acid and are a great source of antioxidants.

Tomatoes are rich in vitamins C and A, both of which fight infections and are essential for immune health. Tomatoes are also famously high in lycopene that protects our skin from ultraviolet damage and oxidative stress, as well as reducing the risk of osteoporosis.

Gluten & dairy free. Vegan friendly.

Yoga Kitchen Buddha Bowls

Within this book you will find the recipes to make up the components of these attractive and delicious Buddha bowls. They are one of my favourite lunches to create from leftovers. The ingredients are listed in the order of assembling of each bowl; in other words the first ingredient listed is the first one to go into the bowl.

Buddha Bowl Serves 1

1 cup of cooked quinoa
½ cup of blanched green peas (frozen is fine)
½ cup of peas shoots (or other micro salad leaves)
1 roasted (in the skin) orange sweet potato
Turmeric & Tahini Dressing see page 36

Gluten, grain & dairy free. Vegan & paleo friendly.

Nourishing Bowl Serves 1

½ cup of micro greens
½ cup of red cabbage, shredded
½ cup of hummus
½ cup of roasted chickpeas (see Roasted Chickpea Salad on page 56)
½ a large avocado
Dress with some cold pressed olive oil, lemon juice and pink salt

Gluten, grain & dairy free. Vegan friendly.

Cleansing Bowl Serves 1

1 small aubergine, washed and sliced, and roasted
3 baby beetroots, washed and halved
½ cup of micro salad leaves
60 g (about 8) fine green beans (blanched or flash boiled)
1 ripe avocado, peeled and sliced
Coriander Pesto (see page 34)
Coriander leaves

Gluten, grain & dairy free. Vegan & paleo friendly.

Glow Bowl Serves 1

½ cup of kale, finely shredded
½ cup of coriander leaves
2 sweet potato medallions (oven roasted)
3–4 spears of tender-stem broccoli (blanched or flash-boiled)
½ cup of cherry tomatoes, sliced in half
⅓ cup of a selection of sprouts (raw)

Gluten, grain & dairy free. Vegan & paleo friendly.

Top left: Buddha Bowl | Top right: Cleansing Bowl | Bottom left: Nourishing Bowl | Bottom right: Glow Bowl

Yoga Kitchen Bowl Serves 1

½ cup of rocket leaves

1 small aubergine, cut into wedges
lengthways

1 courgette, shredded lengthways

¼ cup of sun-dried tomatoes in oil

1 small avocado, peeled and sliced

1 Pea & Jewel Sweet Potato Fritter
(see page 116)

Season the aubergine with salt and roast the pieces in a tablespoon of coconut oil at 180°C for 30 minutes.

Gluten, grain & dairy free. Vegan & paleo friendly.

Korean Bibimbap Bowl Serves 1

½ cup of cooked jasmine rice
(follow package instructions)

½ cup of shitake mushrooms, sautéed

¼ cup of baby spinach, sautéed

¼ of a cucumber, shredded lengthways

2 spring onion stems, finely sliced
lengthways

1 carrot, shredded finely lengthways

1 tbsp tamari sauce

2 tbsp sesame oil

¼ cup of Sriracha sauce

1 tbsp black sesame seeds

Gluten, grain & dairy free. Vegan & paleo friendly.

Summer Rolls Serves 2

Use a combination of at least 2–3 of these ingredients to make up some beautiful, delicious summer rolls.

8 sheets of circular rice papers
1 carrot, shredded lengthways
Avocado, sliced lengthways
Fresh basil leaves
Fresh coriander leaves
Red cabbage, shredded into thin long pieces
Spring onions, sliced finely lengthways

Dipping sauces:
Spicy Peanut Sauce (see page 35)
Harissa Sauce (see page 35)
Sriracha Sauce (a great store-bought option if
you're pressed for time)

Soak one rice sheet at a time in some boiling water for 30 seconds, carefully remove the sheet and place it on a smooth clean cotton tea towel.

Place an eighth of all the ingredients onto the rice sheet. To make up, fold the bottom over. Then fold the sides in. Finally, squeeze and roll to get a nice tight rice paper roll. Then move onto the next sheet and repeat. These are surprisingly filling and 4 per person should be sufficient as a starter or accompaniment to a meal.

Health benefits

These rolls can be filled with a wonderful combination of fresh ingredients that are all packed with fibre, vitamins, minerals and phytonutrients.

Salad Boats

Black Bean, Avocado & Pesto Boats Serves 4

2 heads of baby gem lettuce, stems removed and leaves separated

2 ripe avocados, diced or mashed

1 tin of black beans, rinsed and drained

Coriander Pesto (see page 34)

Wash and dry the gem lettuce leaves thoroughly in a salad spinner.

Mash or slice the avocado with a pinch of salt and a drizzle of cold-pressed olive oil

Next drain and rinse the black beans and then assemble the 'boats' as follows: first add a scoop of black beans to a lettuce leaf and then dress each boat with some pesto and avocado.

Hummus, Pumpkin Seeds & Carrot Boats Serves 4

2 heads of baby gem lettuce, stems removed and leaves separated

½ cup of pumpkin seeds, lightly toasted

2 carrots, shredded finely

Hummus (see recipe on page 37, but store bought is fine too)

Wash and dry the gem lettuce leaves thoroughly in a salad spinner.

Make the hummus if you prefer homemade.

Assemble the boats as follows: first add a scoop of hummus to the lettuce, then the pumpkin seeds, and lastly some carrot.

Health benefits

Black beans are a good source of protein. A low-carb, high-energy bean with plenty of fibre, they are also high in folic acid and magnesium, and a good source of potassium and iron.

Carrots are very high in vitamin A, which is essential for vision and healthy skin and an important protector against infection.

Chickpeas are an excellent source of manganese, magnesium, copper, zinc, and vitamins B1 and B6. They are also rich in dietary fibre, polyunsaturated fatty acids and a great source of plant protein and phytonutrients like quercetin (alleviates bruising oedema, varicose veins, etc.), kaempferol, among many others, all of which protect our bodies against free radical damage and infections that could lead to cancer.

Nourish
& Glow

The Perfect Quinoa Serves 2–4

Quinoa is actually a seed, not a grain, is gluten free, very high in protein and can be wonderfully delicious if cooked with a little love. A cup of dry quinoa yields about 3 cups of cooked quinoa.

1 cup of quinoa (red, white or mixed)
1 cup of water
1 tsp vegetable stock powder
Pinch of pink salt

Rinse and drain the quinoa well.

Toast the quinoa in a dry pot on medium heat for a few minutes, stirring frequently.

When the seeds start to pop it is time to add the water, stock powder and salt.

Allow it to simmer on low heat for approximately 20 minutes with a lid on. Towards the end of the cooking time use a fork to 'fluff' or loosen the quinoa. The quinoa is ready when the seed's 'little leg' appears and all the water has been absorbed.

Serve with plant-based dishes to add protein.

Health benefits

Quinoa (pronounced KEEN-wah) has been cultivated in the Andes for the past 5 thousand years. It has been dubbed 'the mother grain' due to its superfood qualities. Quinoa is technically a seed, not a grain. Quinoa is a **complete protein**, high in iron, magnesium and fibre.

Quinoa is gluten, grain & dairy free. Vegan & paleo friendly.

Roasted Tomato Soup with Cannellini Beans & Pesto *Serves 4*

To turn this into a pasta sauce, omit the stock and beans. Serve over gluten-free spaghetti with pesto drizzled over; my kids adore this over a bowl of pasta.

12 medium-ripe vine tomatoes
2 cloves of garlic, grated
Pink salt and black pepper to taste
1 tsp sugar
1 tsp dried or chopped oregano
3 cups of vegetable stock
4 tbsp tomato paste
2 tins of cannellini beans, drained

Pesto:
1½ cups of fresh basil
1 clove of garlic
½ cup of raw or lightly toasted cashew nuts
Juice of half a small lemon
⅓ cup of cold-pressed olive oil
Good pinch of pink salt

Wash and cut all the tomatoes in half, place them skin down in a greased baking tray. Place them in a 180°C preheated oven and roast them for 40 minutes.

While the tomatoes are roasting, wash and dry the basil, peel and finely grate a garlic clove, and place them into the blender or food processor jug. Now add the cashews, lemon juice, olive oil and salt, and whiz it altogether until you have a pesto of course consistency. Set aside to infuse.

Remove the tomatoes from the oven. Once cooled peel the skins; they should come off very easily.

In a deep soup pot, fry the remaining two grated cloves of garlic and then add the peeled tomato halves as well as the salt, sugar, oregano, stock and tomato paste. Let it all simmer together on the hob for 20 minutes on medium heat, then remove from heat and allow to cool for a few minutes. With a stick blender, blitz it until the soup is smooth and silky. Lastly add the rinsed and drained beans, reheat on the hob for a few minutes and serve with the pesto drizzled on top.

Health benefits

Tomatoes are rich in vitamins C and A, both of which fight infections and are essential for immune health. Tomatoes are also famously high in lycopene that protects our skin from ultraviolet damage and oxidative stress, as well as reducing the risk of osteoporosis. Try and include cooked tomatoes in your diet frequently, as the lycopene content increases with cooking.

Basil is high in vitamins K and A, and beta carotene, and also contains a fair amount of iron, calcium and manganese.

Cannellini beans are low GI, which means that they release energy over a longer period of time. A good source of protein and an excellent source of fibre, these beans are a good source of calcium, copper and iron too.

Grain, gluten & dairy free. Vegan friendly, and can be paleo friendly if beans are omitted.

Dhal Soup with Bhaji Dumplings   Serves 4–6

For a traditional dhal, only add half the stock, and serve it with well-cooked, brown basmati rice. In Ayurveda, dhal is used as a gentle detox food, to be eaten for lunch and dinner for a few days consecutively.

2 medium brown onions, finely chopped
1 tbsp ghee, butter or coconut oil
2 cloves of garlic, crushed
1 tsp each of ground cumin, turmeric and coriander
1 tbsp mild masala
1 tsp pink salt
2 cups of dry, split red lentils
1½ litres vegetable stock
3 large tomatoes, peeled and chopped

Bhaji:
2 brown onions
½ cup of chickpea flour
1 tbsp mild masala
1 tsp pink salt
50 ml water
3 tbsp coconut oil

Garnish:
1 tsp each of cumin seeds, mustard seeds
   and fennel seeds
2 tsp coconut oil
Fresh coriander leaves for garnishing

Fry two of the onions in a deep soup pot in ghee or butter until soft and golden. Then add the crushed garlic and the soup spices, stirring them with the onions for a further minute or two. Now add the dry lentils and stir through the onion-spice mixture, toasting them lightly. After a minute add the stock and chopped tomatoes, and place the lid on the pot and let it simmer for approximately 40 minutes on low heat, stirring occasionally. While the soup is slowly cooking, slice the remaining 2 onions lengthwise for the bhajis. Add them to a mixing bowl together with the chickpea flour, masala and salt, stirring through so that the onions are coated evenly, then add the water (approximately 50 ml will do) and mix well. Heat the coconut oil in a pan, and then, using a tablespoon, scoop dollops of bhaji mixture into the hot oil. They need to be golden and crispy on all sides and it's best to pay close attention to them as they cook so you can turn them as needed.

Lastly, heat a little coconut oil in a sauce pan and add the spice seeds. Fry them for approximately a minute, and serve sprinkled over the soup. Garnish with coriander leaves.

Health benefits

Lentils are an excellent source of folic acid, iron, protein and healthy dietary fibre. It becomes a complete protein meal when paired with a wholegrain like brown rice.

This soup also contains healing spices like **turmeric** (turmeric is an anti-inflammatory and fights many types of cancer), **cumin** (aids digestion and protects the body against the effects of stress), **fennel** (treats flatulence and aids in digestion) and **coriander leaves** (aids the body in eliminating heavy metals and is also antibacterial).

Gluten, grain & dairy free (if you use coconut oil).

Carrot & Peanut Soup Serves 4

This soup is perfect as a starter or for a light lunch. Use organic carrots as their nutritional value is much higher and they are usually very affordable. Use unsweetened, non-GMO peanut butter, available at most supermarkets in their health food section, or from your local health store.

650 g medium carrots

1 tbsp coconut oil

2 small red onions, finely sliced

3 cloves of garlic

1 tbsp fresh ginger, finely grated

3 cups of vegetable stock

1 400g tin of coconut milk

2 tbsp Thai red curry paste

1 tsp turmeric powder

Salt to taste

2 tbsp peanut butter

Large roasted peanuts & spicy chilli sauce to garnish (optional)

Wash, peel and cut the carrots into 4-cm-thick slices. In a soup pot, heat some coconut oil, fry the onions until soft and then add the carrots, crushed garlic and ginger and fry, stirring frequently for a further 5 minutes.

Then add the stock, coconut milk, red curry paste, turmeric and salt and cook together for 35 minutes. Remove the soup from the heat and let it cool for 2 minutes, then add the peanut butter and blitz with a hand blender until you have silky smooth consistency.

Serve with a drizzle of chilli sauce (optional), and garnish with roasted peanuts.

Health benefits

Carrots are very high in vitamin A, essential for vision and healthy skin and an important protector against infection; vitamin C, essential for immune health and collagen production; vitamin K, vitamin B8, panthogenic acid, folic acid (folate), potassium, iron, copper and manganese. Carrots are also a powerhouse of fibre that is essential for good digestive health.

Peanuts are a good source of protein, vitamin E, niacin, folic acid and manganese.

Gluten, grain & dairy free. Vegan & paleo friendly.

Bone Broth

Bone broth is basically an old-fashioned stock, cooked for anything from 2–48 hours (don't turn the page yet!). See below some of the benefits of broth.

You can use many different kinds of bones for making broth. I like beef short rib, oxtail and any 'soup bones' your butcher has on offer. If you are in a hurry, or do not have a pressure or slow cooker, you can also use the bones from free-range/organic chicken. Chicken bones will yield a mineral-rich broth faster than the hard beef bones. I can recommend using a pressure cooker if you have one; alternatively you can make use of an eco-cooking sack, like a Wonderbag, so that the first 8 hours is on your stovetop and the remaining overnight time is in the bag. To make bone broth, you need a large stock pot or pressure cooker, a strainer and a muslin cloth (optional).

Use approximately 750g (or more) beef bones and/or the bones from 1 or 2 roast chickens
1 yellow/brown onion, chopped roughly
3 stalks of celery, chopped roughly
2 medium carrots, chopped roughly
2 bay leaves
30 ml apple cider vinegar
Pink salt (1 tsp or more to taste)

Add all the bone broth ingredients into your stock pot/pressure cooker then fill it with water to cover the ingredients by at least 5 cm. Bring to the boil and then turn down to simmer on low heat for 8–10 hours in the pot. Next transfer it to the eco sack for overnight slow cooking. Or alternately cook it for approx 3–4 hours in the pressure cooker, but make sure that only 2/3 of the pressure cooker is filled for safety reasons.

Once cooked sufficiently pour the broth through a strainer (and additionally a muslin cloth for a clearer broth) and use immediately to make soup, or you can freeze it in batches to add to stews, risotto & soups at a later time.

Health benefits

Helps seal & heal your gut.
Helps the body fight infection.
Reduces joint pain and inflammation.
Promotes strong healthy bones.
Promotes healthy hair, and nail growth.

Hearty Bone Broth Vegetable Soup

Serve on a cold winter's day with a generous drizzle of olive oil and some cayenne pepper to get your blood flowing and your sinuses open. This soup is an excellent cold and flu remedy.

1 litre bone broth
1 stalk of celery with leaves
3 carrots, grated
2 yellow or brown onions
4 medium courgettes, grated
2 cups of chopped kale or spinach
1 tbsp of vegetable stock powder
1 sprig of thyme
1 sprig of oregano
3 cloves of garlic
½ cup of red split lentils
½ cup of split peas
Salt and black pepper to taste

In a deep soup pot, add all the veggies and herbs to the pre-cooked broth and let it simmer over low heat for approximately 1 hour.

Gluten, grain & dairy free. Can be made paleo friendly if you omit the split peas and lentils.

Spiced Pumpkin Soup Serves 4-6

2 queen squash/pumpkins, or 2 small
butternuts

1 red onion, finely sliced

1 tbsp coconut oil

2 cloves of garlic, freshly crushed

1 heaped tbsp mild masala

1 tsp turmeric powder

1 tsp ground coriander

1 tsp pink salt

2½ cups of vegetable stock

1 tin of coconut milk

Preheat the oven to 180°C, then slice the squashes in half (the butternuts will be have to be sliced lengthways), and add them with the pips and pulp still in them face down on to a greased baking tray and transfer them to the oven to roast for 45 minutes.

In a deep soup pot, fry the sliced onion in the coconut oil until they are soft, adding next the crushed garlic and all the spices, and sauté for a further 3 minutes.

When the squashes are soft and fully roasted, remove them from the oven and let them cool enough to handle, scooping out the pips and pulp and discarding it, and then scoop out the flesh into the pot with the onions and spices. Add the salt, vegetable stock and coconut milk and bring it all to a gentle simmer for 10 minutes.

Remove the soup from the heat, giving it 5 minutes' cooling time and then using a hand blender whiz it into a smooth silky soup. Serve with a drizzle of olive oil, ground black pepper and some fresh coriander (optional).

Health benefits

Squash is very rich in fibre as well as containing excellent amounts of vitamins A, C, B6 and B3 as well as minerals such as manganese, copper, potassium and folic acid. Squash also contains good amounts of omega-3 fatty acids.

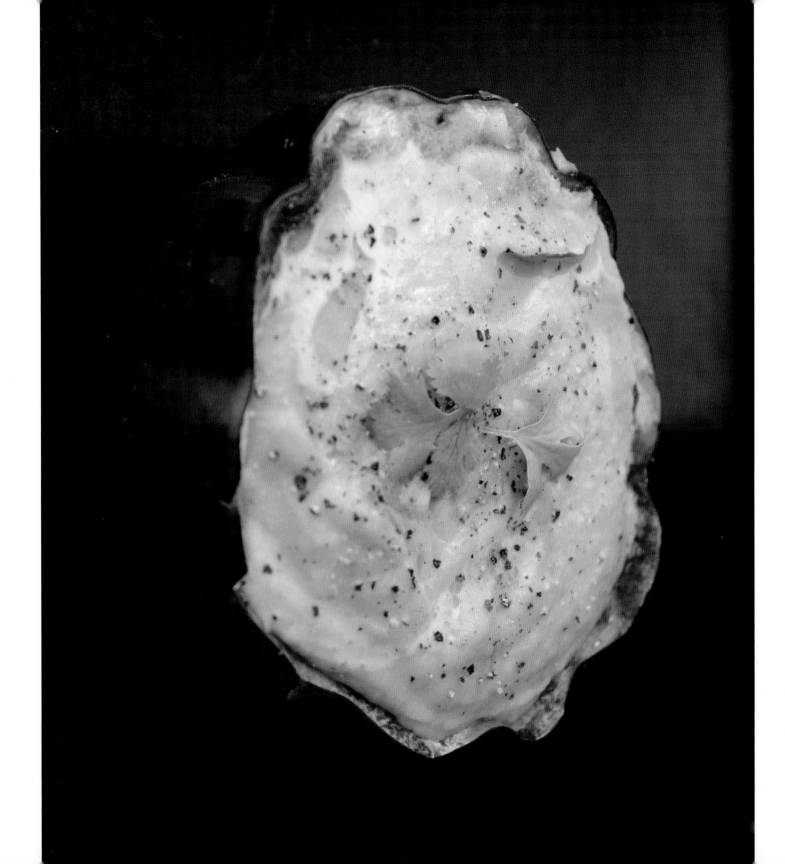

Aubergine & Tomato Curry Serves 4

Serve this curry with quinoa or alternatively with poached fish (hake works well) to make it a carb-free flexitarian meal.

3 large aubergines
Coconut oil
2 medium brown onions, sliced
3 cloves of garlic, finely chopped
1 small knob of ginger, finely chopped
1 tbsp mild masala
1 tsp each of turmeric, cumin and coriander powders and paprika
1 heaped tsp each of cumin and mustard seeds
1 pinch cinnamon powder
1 heaped tsp pink salt
2 cardamom pods
6 medium tomatoes, coursely chopped
100 ml water
Fresh coriander leaves for garnishing (optional)

Cut the aubergines into large chunks (4cm x 4cm), then place them on a baking tray. Season with salt and add two tablespoons of melted coconut oil; mix well so that all the pieces have a coating of oil. Pop into a preheated oven to roast/bake for 30 minutes at 180°C.

While the aubergines are roasting, sauté the onions in a teaspoon of coconut oil until they are soft and golden. Then add the garlic and ginger, as well as all the spices, frying for a further 3 minutes on low heat. Add the tomatoes and water to the spices and onions and cook on low heat, stirring occasionally for a further 20 minutes. Then add the roasted aubergines to the tomato, onion and spice sauce and let it all simmer together, with the lid on, for another 10 minutes.

Serve with quinoa or brown basmati rice.

Health benefits

Aubergines, also known as eggplant or brinjal, have an impressive spectrum of nutrients in them: fibre, folic acid, potassium, manganese, as well as vitamins C, K and B6, phosphorous, copper, thiamine, niacin, magnesium and pantothenic acid.

The phytonutrient nasunin in the skin of the aubergine is a powerful antioxidant that protects brain cells against free radical damage.

Tomatoes also have a wide variety of healthful nutrients like vitamins A, C (to fight infections) and K, potassium (controlling heart rate and blood pressure), manganese and vitamin E, thiamine, niacin, vitamin B6 and folic acid, magnesium and phosphorus.

Gluten & dairy free.

Vegan Thai Red Curry Serves 4

Serve this curry with quinoa for an extra boost of protein.

1 small knob of ginger, finely grated
2 cloves of garlic, freshly crushed or grated
1 red pepper, sliced into ribbons
1 yellow pepper, sliced into ribbons
2 small courgettes, sliced
Handful of mini corn, whole
Handful of mange tout, whole
Handful of tender-stem broccoli, whole
4 spring onions, thickly sliced
2 tbsp smooth peanut butter
2 tbsp tamari or soy sauce
2 tbsp red curry paste
1 400g tin of coconut milk
Coriander leaves and roasted peanuts
for garnish (optional)

Stir-fry the garlic and ginger together with the peppers and sliced courgettes for approximately 5 minutes, and then add the corn, mange tout, broccoli and spring onions.

Stir-fry for a few more minutes and then add all the remaining ingredients and allow it to simmer on low heat for 15–20 minutes, stirring occasionally.

Garnish with chopped coriander leaves and crushed, roasted peanuts.

Health benefits

Yellow & red pepper have more than twice the vitamin C of oranges, which makes them excellent immune boosters. They also lower inflammation in the arteries that lead to heart disease. The sulphur content in peppers makes them effective in fighting cancer while the lutein content helps protect eyes from cataracts and macular degeneration in later life.

Tender-stem broccoli is also classified as a superfood, for it is high in iron and vitamin C, and is full of cancer-fighting phytonutrients and antioxidants, most important of which is sulforaphane, which plays a large role in immune, eye and heart health.

Quinoa with Roasted Vegetables & Wilted Spinach Serves 4–6

This recipe is perfect to make ahead and store in the fridge for healthy packed lunches.

6 baby beetroot

3 red onions

8 white mushrooms

2 jewel (orange flesh) sweet potatoes

3 medium vine tomatoes

2 cups of chopped baby spinach leaves

2 cups of cooked quinoa (see page 72)

Salt and pepper to taste

Coconut oil

Peel and quarter the baby beetroot and onions; de-stem and halve the mushrooms; wash the sweet potatoes thoroughly with a vegetable brush, leaving the peel on, then slice into 5-cm-thick medallions; wash and halve the tomatoes.

Spread the vegetables on a large baking tray, generously greased with coconut oil. Roast them for approximately 40–50 minutes in a 180°C preheated oven. Check on the tomatoes and onions after 35 minutes, and remove them if they are ready.

Toss the raw, chopped baby spinach through the hot quinoa to get the 'wilted' effect, and then serve the roasted vegetables on top of the quinoa and spinach.

Season with salt, freshly ground pepper, a generous drizzle with truffle oil or good cold pressed olive oil.

Health benefits

Quinoa is a complete protein with a cup of it containing 8 g of protein. Quinoa has twice as much fibre as most grains, although technically it is a seed. It is also rich in manganese, magnesium, phosphorus, zinc, iron and copper.

Sweet potatoes, the orange flesh variety, are one of nature's unsurpassed sources of beta carotene, which converts into vitamin A in the body. It is helpful to include some fat with a sweet potato meal as this will increase your body's beta carotene uptake. Sweet potatoes also have anti-inflammatory properties, can assist in curing stomach ulcers and can provide relief from arthritis. They are also rich in vitamins C, B1 and B2, are a good source of biotin, potassium and an excellent source of fibre.

Beets stimulate liver function, help prevent skin, lung and colon cancer, boost the immune system and contribute to heart health. Beets are rich in folic acid, vitamins C and B6, thiamin, manganese, potassium, magnesium and copper.

Grain, gluten & dairy free. Vegan & paleo friendly.

Best Chickpea Curry Serves 4-6

This curry is a staple in our house. Serve with a fresh chutney and quinoa or rice, or my Mung Bean & Cauliflower Curry (see page 98) for a vegan curry feast.

1 cup of dry chickpeas, soaked overnight
   or 2 400 g tins of chickpeas
3 medium brown onions, chopped
1 tbsp coconut oil
2 cloves of garlic, grated or crushed
1 tbsp grated ginger
100 ml water
2 whole cloves
2 cardamom pods
5 curry leaves
1 tsp each of ground turmeric, ground
   coriander, cumin seeds and fennel seeds
1 tbsp mild garam masala
6 medium tomatoes, chopped
1 tsp pink salt
1 tsp black pepper

Begin by draining and then cooking the soaked chickpeas in well salted water for 30–40 minutes, then drain and set aside.

While the chickpeas are cooking, sauté the onions in coconut oil until they are soft and golden. Add the minced garlic and ginger, as well as all the spices, frying for a further 3 minutes on low heat.

Now add the chopped tomatoes, stirring frequently until the tomatoes become soft and cooked. Add the water, place the lid on the pot and let it simmer for approximately 15 minutes.

Then add the cooked chickpeas and season with salt and pepper. Stir through and let the curry cook on low heat for a further 20 minutes.

Health benefits

Chickpeas are an excellent source of manganese, magnesium, copper, zinc and vitamins B1 & B6. They are also rich in dietary fibre, polyunsaturated fatty acids and a great source of plant protein and phytonutrients like quercetin and kaempferol that alleviate bruising oedema and varicose veins, and many other phytonutrients that protect our bodies against free radical damage and infections that could lead to cancer.

Curcumin in **turmeric** is a superfood, which encourages the gallbladder to produce bile which improves digestion. It is a powerful anti-inflammatory and can help diminish the symptoms of osteoarthritis and rheumatic conditions. Turmeric can assist in preventing a number of cancers including breast, colon, prostrate and skin.

Garlic protects against stomach cancer, lowers cholesterol in the blood, helps to prevent blood clots and is an excellent immune booster.

Ginger reduces nausea and can help in the prevention and treatment of arthritis, asthma, certain cancers, heartburn and indigestion.

Gluten, grain & dairy free. Vegan friendly.

Portobello Bun Burger Serves 4

8 large Portobello mushrooms

Pink salt to taste

Pea & Jewel Sweet Potato Fritter
(see page 116)

1 avocado

Harissa Paste (see page 35)

De-stem and season the mushrooms with pink salt, place them on a baking sheet, and transfer them to a 180°C preheated oven for 20 minutes.

While they are roasting, prepare the fritter batter and begin to shallow frying the fritters in 2 batches. Once the mushrooms are roasted, assemble the burgers using the mushroom as the 'burger bun', and the fritter as the 'patty', add some avocado and Harrissa paste to spice it up.

Dressed Up Mushrooms Serve at least 2–3 mushrooms per person as a starter portion

Small- to medium-sized Portobello
mushrooms

Harrissa Paste (see page 35)

Coriander Pesto (see page 34)

Hummus (see page 37)

Mashed avocado

Vine tomatoes

Soft goats' cheese

Toasted sesame seeds

Prepare the mushrooms by seasoning them with salt and trimming their stems if necessary. Place them in a roasting pan and pop them in a 180°C preheated oven for 20 minutes. Remove and let them cool.

Then start creating delicious, beautiful toppings for each of the roasted mushrooms:

– Harissa paste & mashed avocado with a sprinkling of sesame seeds

– Goats cheese, pesto & thin slices of tomato

– Hummus & sliced tomato

– Coriander pesto & avocado

Health benefits

Portobello mushrooms are a good source of plant protein with lots of fibre and are low in carbohydrates, making them a great addition to a weight-loss eating plan. Portobello mushrooms are also high in phosphorus, B-vitamins, copper and selenium.

Avocados are a superfood rich in vitamin K and C, folic acid and panthothenic acid, minerals such as potassium, copper, manganese and magnesium. It is packed with fibre and are also full of anti-aging antioxidants. They also aid in digestion.

Gluten & grain free. Paleo & vegan friendly (if goat's cheese is omitted).

Bean Chilli Serves 4–6

2 red onions, finely chopped
1 tbsp coconut oil
1 red pepper, diced
3 carrots, grated
1 stick of celery, finely diced
1 tbsp ground cumin
1 tbsp cumin seeds
1 tbsp sweet paprika
1 tsp ground coriander
1 pinch of smoked paprika
 (optional)
1 bay leaf

1 pinch of cinnamon
3 cloves of garlic, crushed or finely grated
5 medium tomatoes, chopped
1 tbsp tomato puree
½ tsp sugar
Pink salt
1 cup of dry black beans, soaked overnight
 and cooked in salted water
 or 2 400 g tins of black beans, drained well
1 cup of shredded kale or spinach (tightly packed)
Avocado & chopped coriander leaves for
 garnishing (optional)

Fry the onions until soft, then add the red pepper, carrots, celery, spices and garlic, frying them all together for a further 10 minutes.

Next add the tomatoes, tomato paste, sugar and salt, the black beans and the shredded spinach, and then allow it to simmer together for approximately 20 minutes.

Serve with brown rice or quinoa, avocado and chopped fresh coriander.

Health benefits

Black beans are a good source of protein. A low-carb, high-energy bean with plenty of fibre, they are also high in folic acid and magnesium, and a good source of potassium and iron.

Carrots are high in vitamin A, essential for vision and healthy skin and an important protector against infection.

Celery is rich in a wide variety of vitamins and minerals. They are rich in potassium and vitamin K, as well as various other phytonutrients like lutein and zeaxanthin that are reported to lower inflammation.

Red bell peppers have more than twice the vitamin C of oranges, which make them excellent immune boosters. They lower inflammation in the arteries that lead to heart disease.

Tomatoes are rich in vitamins A and C (to fight infections) and K, potassium (controlling heart rate & blood pressure), manganese and vitamin E, thiamine, niacin, vitamin B6 and folate, magnesium and phosphorus.

Gluten, grain & dairy free. Vegan friendly.

Monica's Mushroom Bolognaise Serves 4–6

My friend Monica is one of the kindest and sweetest people I know, and a wonderful cook too. She made this for me one cold winter evening when I was tired and hungry and it was comforting and delicious. Since then it has become a fabulously messy favourite in our house.

1 brown onion, chopped

1 tbsp coconut oil

2 cloves of garlic, grated or crushed

2 large carrots, grated

3 large Portobello mushrooms, de-stemmed and coarsely grated

1 400 g jar of passata (pulped tomatoes)

1 tsp ground coriander

1 tsp paprika

1 sprig each of oregano and basil, chopped finely (if using dried herbs, 1 tsp of each)

½ tsp brown sugar

Salt to taste

2 tbsp nutritional yeast flakes

1 tbsp vegetable stock powder

1 500 g packet of dried spaghetti (gluten-free, or ordinary)

Parmesan cheese to serve (optional)

Fry the onions in coconut oil in a large pot until soft and translucent. Then add the garlic, carrot and mushrooms. Season with salt to taste and stir-fry the veggies for a further 10 minutes.

Then add the pasata, all the herbs and spices, as well as the nutritional yeast and stock powder and salt to taste. Stir through and let it simmer gently without a lid on, stirring occasionally, for 20 minutes.

Serve over cooked spaghetti with a generous drizzle of olive oil, some freshly ground black pepper and a sprinkle of some more nutritional yeast, or Parmesan cheese.

Health benefits

Portobello mushrooms are a good source of plant protein with lots of fibre, and are low in carbohydrates, making them a great addition to a weight-loss eating plan. They are also high in phosphorus, B-vitamins, copper and selenium.

Pulped tomatoes are high in vitamins A and C, and are high in lycopene.

Can be gluten free if you use gluten-free pasta. Dairy free & vegan friendly (if you omit the cheese).

Mung Beans & Cauliflower

1 head of cauliflower

½ tsp turmeric

½ cup of dry mung beans

2 cardamom pods

Fresh chutney:

2 large tomatoes, roughly chopped

1 clove of garlic, freshly crushed

1 small red onion, roughly chopped

3 tbsp olive oil

½ cup of fresh coriander leaves

½ tsp pink salt

Whizz all the chutney ingredients together in a food processor or blender, until you have a runny but course consistency.

Separate and wash the cauliflower florets. Place them on a greased baking tray, season with salt and dust them with the turmeric. Allow them roast for 20 minutes in a 180°C preheated oven.

While the cauliflower is roasting, bring the mung beans to boil in plenty of salted water, together with the whole cardamom pods to infuse them with their flavour. They will need approximately 30–35 minutes to cook. Drain them and add them to a serving bowl, together with the roasted cauliflower florets, and lastly add the fresh chutney in dollops here and there.

Serve along side the Aubergine & Tomato Curry (see page 84) or the Chickpea Curry (see page 90).

Health benefits

Mung beans are a good source of plant-based protein, as well as fibre, vitamins A, B, D and E, as well as calcium, potassium, iron, zinc and magnesium.

Cauliflower is an excellent source of fibre, vitamins C, K and B6, folic acid, choline and omega-3 fatty acids.

Baked Tofu & Veggie Rice Serves 4–6

¾ cup of brown basmati rice
1 tbsp vegetable stock powder
Pink salt to taste
1 400 g block of firm, plain tofu
1 tbsp coconut oil
1 tsp honey
1 tbsp teriyaki sauce
2 carrots, grated
1 red pepper, diced
2 cloves of garlic, freshly crushed
1 cup of frozen peas
Chopped spring onion to garnish (optional)

Sauce:

1 tbsp teriyaki sauce
2 tbsp sesame oil
1 tsp honey
a pinch of pink salt

Whisk all the sauce ingredients together.

Start by cooking the brown basmati rice with the vegetable stock powder and a good pinch of pink salt added to the water. Brown basmati rice needs at least 40–50 minutes of cooking on low heat with a lid on (when adding the water to the uncooked rice, make sure there should be about 1½ cm of water above the surface of the rice).

Slice the tofu into thick slices of about 12 mm, then place them flat on a baking tray greased with coconut oil. Whisk the teaspoon of honey and the tablespoon of teriyaki sauce together in a bowl and then drizzle it over the tofu slices, making sure that the sauce is coated evenly over the tofu pieces. Place the tofu slices in a 170°C preheated oven for 20 minutes.

While the tofu is baking, sauté the grated carrot, diced red pepper and crushed garlic together in a little coconut oil for about 15 minutes on medium heat. Add the peas approximately 5 minutes before the end to thaw and cook through.

Lastly, stir the sautéed veggies through the cooked basmati rice. Serve the rice in a bowl with a wedge of roasted tofu and a drizzle of the sauce.

Health benefits

Tofu is a good source of protein, containing all eight essential amino acids. Tofu is also rich in vitamin B1, magnesium, zinc, copper, iron and calcium and other micronutrients. It should be eaten in moderation as it increases oestrogen levels in the body.

Gluten & dairy free. Vegan friendly.

Bean & Tomato Stew with Polenta

¾ cup of non-GMO course polenta

1 tablespoon of coconut oil

1 large red onion, finely sliced

1 400g jar of tomato & basil pasta sauce

1 tsp thyme

1 tsp ground coriander

Pink salt to taste

2 cloves of garlic

1 tin of kidney beans

1 400g tin of butter beans

Black pepper

Cook the polenta in salted water according to the package instructions.

Fry the onion in some coconut oil until it is soft and translucent, then add the jar of tomato pasta sauce, spices, salt and crushed garlic and let it simmer over medium heat for 10 minutes. Next add the rinsed and thoroughly drained beans, stirring them gently through the sauce, and let it simmer for a further 5 minutes before serving.

Serve this hearty, comforting bean stew over the polenta and finish it with a good drizzle of olive oil and a grinding of black pepper before tucking in.

Health benefits

Polenta is a good source of B vitamins, vitamin A and zinc. Polenta has plenty of fibre, is low GI and additionally is gluten free. Make sure you choose non-GMO polenta though.

Beans are a great source of plant protein, fibre, phytonutrients and minerals such as iron, copper, manganese, potassium and folic acid.

Lentil Shepherd's Pie Serves 4–6

1 tablespoon of vegetable stock powder

2 cups of water

1 brown onion, chopped fine

1 tbsp coconut oil

3 large carrots, grated

1 cup of tightly packed spinach, shredded

1 tsp ground coriander

Pinch of ground nutmeg & ground clove each

1 clove of garlic

½ tsp celery salt

1½ cups of dry green or brown lentils

1 sprig of thyme or 1 tsp dried thyme

1 small sprig of oregano or 1 tsp dried oregano

1 tsp mixed herbs

1 tsp sweet paprika

3 large potatoes, peeled and halved

3 jewel (orange flesh) sweet potatoes, peeled and halved

2 tbsp olive oil

Pink salt to taste

4 tbsp nutritional yeast flakes to garnish

Dissolve the vegetable stock powder in the 2 cups of water.

Sauté the finely chopped onion in coconut oil until it is soft and translucent, preferably in a cast iron or oven-proof pot.

Then add the carrot and spinach to the onions and stir-fry for approximately 5 minutes over medium heat. Add the ground spices, garlic, celery salt and lentils, stirring continuously over low heat for another 5 minutes. Lastly, add the vegetable stock, salt and herbs, then place the lid on the pot and let it simmer over low heat for 30 minutes until the lentils are soft and have absorbed most of the stock.

While the lentil mixture simmers happily, peel, halve and cook the potatoes and sweet potatoes in salted water. Once cooked through, mash them with olive oil and salt. Add some of the cooking water to the mash if it seems too dry.

Layer the mash evenly over the lentil base and then pop it under the grill for a few minutes to achieve that crispy top layer and lastly, sprinkle the nutritional yeast before serving.

Health benefits

Lentils are an excellent source of folic acid and iron, protein and healthy dietary fibre.

Spinach is high in niacin, zinc, iron, magnesium, calcium, protein, fibre, vitamin B6, folic acid.

Sweet potatoes are rich in vitamins C, B1 and B2, a good source of biotin and potassium and an excellent source of fibre.

Gluten, grain & dairy free. Vegan friendly.

Amazing Vegetable Bake Serves 6

This veggie bake is sublime, and worth very bit of extra kitchen time it takes to prepare. Crammed with vegetable goodness, it can easily be turned into a gluten-free dish. Make two at a time and freeze one to take care of a fuss-free weeknight dinner.

2 medium aubergines
4 large courgettes
Salt
Coconut oil

Tomato & mushroom sauce:
1 tbsp coconut oil
2 cloves of garlic
1 bunch of spring onions
1 red pepper, finely diced
2 large Portobello mushrooms, de-stemmed and grated
1 50 g sachet of tomato paste, or 3 sundried tomatoes, soaked and blitzed in a blender

750 ml Italian passata
1 tsp brown sugar
Pink salt to taste
1 tsp ground cumin
1 tsp dried or fresh chopped mint
1 tsp sweet paprika
a pinch of smoked paprika
2–3 tbsp coconut oil

'Cheese' sauce:
3 tbsp butter (or to make it vegan, coconut oil)
3 tbsp all-purpose flour (or gluten-free flour

500 ml almond or ordinary milk (I use almond, but ordinary will do if you don't have an issue with dairy)
3 tbsp nutritional yeast flakes
½ tsp turmeric
1 tbsp olive oil
1 tsp vegetable stock powder
1 tsp garlic salt

½ cup of mature cheddar cheese or vegan cheese, grated

Tomato Sauce: Using the coconut oil, fry the crushed garlic, finely sliced spring onions and finely chopped red pepper in a large cast-iron pot or skillet, then add the grated mushroom and stir fry for about 5 minutes. Add the tomato pulp and puree, brown sugar, salt and all the sauce spices. Stir through and then let it simmer.

'Cheese' Sauce: On low heat in a large sauce pan, mix the butter or coconut oil with the flour, then add the almond milk gradually until you have a smooth mixture. Turn the heat up and stirring continuously, add all the other 'cheese' sauce ingredients. Gently let it simmer, stirring the whole time until it has thickened.

Veggie layer: Top and tail the aubergines and courgettes. Slice them lengthways as thinly as possible. Season the slices with salt and fry them in coconut oil in batches until partially cooked on low heat in a pan.

Oil an oven-proof dish well, and then layer as follows:

Layer the aubergine slices along the base and sides of the dish – they should overlap one another – then half the tomato and mushroom sauce. Next add a layer of courgette, overlapping slightly, and then a layer of 'cheese' sauce.

Now add the other half of the tomato and mushroom sauce, and again a layer of aubergines and courgettes, mixed this time, leaving a gap here and there for the sauce to bubble though.

Lastly pour the remaining 'cheese sauce' and top with the grated cheese if using.

Pop into the oven and let it bake for a good 45 minutes in a 180°C preheated oven.

Health benefits:

Portobello mushrooms are a good source of plant protein with lots of fibre. Low in carbohydrates, it is a great addition to a weight-loss eating plan. Portobello mushrooms are also high in phosphorus, B vitamins, copper and selenium.

Aubergines, also known as eggplant or brinjal, have an impressive spectrum of nutrients in them: fibre, folate, potassium, manganese, as well as vitamins C, K and B6, phosphorous, copper, thiamine, niacin, magnesium and pantothenic acid. The phytonutrient nasunin, found in the skin of the aubergine, is a powerful antioxidant that protects brain cells against free radical damage.

Courgettes, also known as zucchini, are rich in B-complex vitamins, choline, as well as minerals such as zinc, magnesium, iron and phosphorous.

Dairy free, and can be gluten free if using gluten-free flour. Vegan friendly.

Aubergine 'Pizza' Serves 4–6

2 medium-to-large aubergines

2 tbsp coconut oil

½ tsp pink salt

1 400 g jar of good pasta sauce (basil infused
is a good choice)

½ cup of coriander or basil pesto (see page 34
for Coriander Pesto recipe)

Wash, remove the stem, and slice the aubergines lengthways into 1-cm-thick pieces, sprinkle them with salt and then place them on a baking tray greased with coconut oil in a 180°C preheated oven for 25–30 minutes.

Spread a generous helping of pasta sauce and return them to the oven for a further 10–15 minutes. Serve with a drizzle of pesto.

Health benefits

Aubergines, also known as eggplant or brinjal, have an impressive spectrum of nutrients in them, fibre, folic acid, potassium, manganese, as well as vitamins C, K and B6, phosphorous, copper, thiamine, niacin, magnesium and pantothenic acid. The phytonutrient nasunin, found in its skin, is a powerful antioxidant that protects brain cells against free radical damage.

Tomatoes also have wide variety of healthy nutrients like vitamins A, C (to fight infections) and K, potassium (to control heart rate and blood pressure), manganese and vitamin E, thiamine, niacin, vitamin B6 and folic acid, magnesium and phosphorus.

Stuffed Butternut with Roasted Chickpeas Serves 4

2 small butternuts, halved lengthways,
    pips removed
1 400 g tin of chickpeas, rinsed and
    drained well
Pink salt to taste
Coconut oil
1 tsp ground cumin
100 g or 2 discs of feta cheese, crumbled
¾ cup baby spinach, shredded
2 tbsp Tahini Paste (see page 36)
30 ml water
1 tsp garlic salt

Preheat the oven to 170°C. Place the halved butternuts, face down, on a greased baking tin or oven-proof dish in the oven, and roast them for about 40–50 minutes.

Season the chickpeas with salt, add a tablespoon of coconut oil and place them on a separate baking tin or ovenproof dish. Roast them for 15 minutes in the oven. During their roasting, they require a good shake to get all the sides roasted and coated with oil evenly.

While the butternut and chickpeas are roasting, mix the feta and raw, shredded spinach well and prepare the sauce by simply whisking all its ingredients together well.

Once the butternut halves are ready, remove them from the oven and stuff them with the spinach and feta. Sprinkle over the roasted chickpeas and drizzle them with the sauce. Voila, you are ready to serve.

Health benefits

Butternut is extremely high in vitamin A, which is an essential antioxidant. It is also a good source of vitamins C, E and B6, and is a fair source of minerals such as zinc, iron, calcium, magnesium and manganese. Butternut also contains the phytonutrients, carotene-b and lutein.

Grain & gluten free. Can be paleo friendly if chickpeas are omitted, and vegan friendly if the feta is.

Stuffed Peppers Serves 4

4 red or yellow peppers
1 tbsp coconut oil
2 large carrots, grated
2 medium courgettes, grated
1 tsp ground cumin
½ tsp paprika
Salt to taste
2 cups of cooked red quinoa

Sauce:
½ cup of baby spinach, washed and dried
⅓ cup of fresh coriander, washed and dried
3 tbsp olive oil
1 clove of garlic, crushed
Salt to taste

Halve the peppers lengthways and remove the stems, flesh and pips. Place them, face down, on a baking sheet greased with coconut oil in a 180°C preheated oven for 30 minutes.

While the peppers are roasting, stir-fry the carrots and courgettes in coconut oil with the spices and a pinch of salt for about 10 minutes.

Add the sauce ingredients to your food processor or blender and pulse until you have a smooth consistency.

Mix the vegetables and quinoa together and stuff the peppers with this mixture. Drizzle over the spinach and coriander sauce and serve.

Health benefits

Red Bell Peppers have more than twice the vitamin C of oranges, which makes them excellent immune boosters. They also lower inflammation in the arteries that lead to heart disease. The sulphur content in peppers make them effective in fighting cancer, and the lutein content helps to protect eyes from cataracts and macular degeneration in later life.

Gluten, grain & dairy free. Vegan & paleo friendly.

Crispy Things

Pakoras Serves 6

Serve these with fresh chutney (see Mung Beans & Cauliflower on page 98) alongside the Aubergine & Tomato Curry (see page 84), or serve them as part of a vegetarian starter platter.

⅓ cup of chickpea flour
1 tbsp mild masala
½ tsp turmeric
1 tsp pink salt
½ tsp bicarbonate of soda
¾ cup of grated aubergine
½ cup of grated courgette
½ cup of grated potato
¼ cup of water
3 tbsp coconut oil for shallow frying

In a large mixing bowl, mix the chickpea flour, spices, salt and bicarbonate well, then add all the grated vegetables and the water, and stir it well so that everything is covered with flour and spices.

Now form the batter into golf-size balls, pressing down slightly before carefully dropping them into the hot coconut oil. Fry until they are golden and crispy on both sides, turning only once.

Onion Bhajis Serves 4–6

Serve these as dumplings with a dhal or the Dhal Soup (see page 76) as they add the needed crunch and flavours to complement those curries.

⅓ cup of chickpea flour
½ tsp turmeric
1 tsp ground coriander
1 tbsp mild masala
1 tsp pink salt
Pinch of bicarbonate of soda
3 medium red onions, thinly sliced
⅕ cup water
3 tbsp coconut oil for shallow frying

In a large mixing bowl, mix the chickpea flour, spices, salt and bicarbonate of soda well, then add all the finely sliced onions and the water and stir it well so that all of the onion is covered with flour and spices. Carefully drop spoonfuls of batter into the hot coconut oil. Fry until they are golden and crispy on both sides, turning only once.

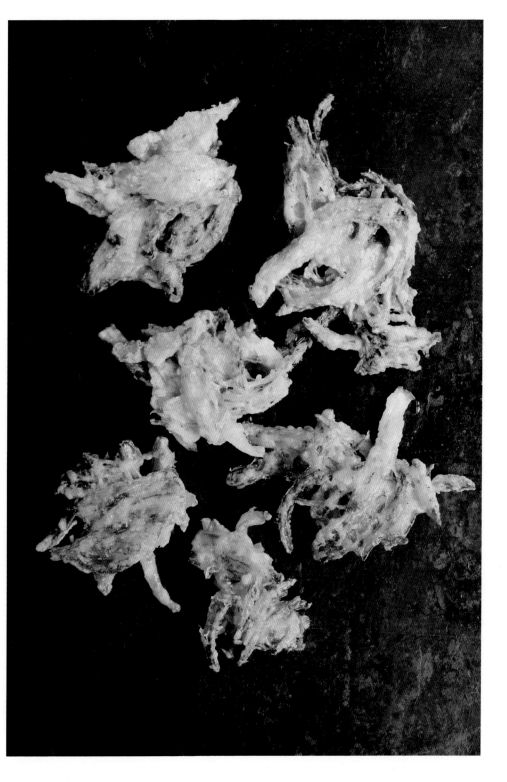

Onion Bhajis

Health benefits

The phytonutrients in **onions** improve the working of vitamin C, adding another layer to the body's immunity. Onions also contain chromium that regulates blood sugar, so adding a few rings of onion to meals is a good idea if you are trying to lose weight. Onions are also rich in quercetin, an antioxidant rumoured to act like a natural anti-histamine, so if you suffer from allergies why not try a diet abundant in onions.

Gluten, grain & dairy free. Vegan friendly.

(continued of following page)

Carrot & Sweet Corn Fritters Serves 4

Serve these as a side to a salad at lunch, or use them to replace a meat patty for a 'veggie' burger (see page 92). They go particularly well with tangy coleslaw (see page 46).

½ cup of gluten-free flour or unbleached
   wheat flour
½ cup of grated carrot
½ cup of frozen sweet corn, thawed
½ tsp paprika
½ tsp cumin
½ tsp cayenne pepper
½ tsp bicarbonate of soda
Salt to taste
2–3 tablespoons of coconut oil
Sliced spring onion, to garnish (optional

Pea & Jewel Sweet Potato Fritters

½ cup of gluten-free flour or unbleached
   wheat flour
½ tsp paprika
½ tsp cumin
½ tsp cayenne pepper
½ tsp bicarbonate of soda
Salt to taste
½ cup of jewel (orange flesh) sweet potato,
   grated
½ cup of frozen baby green peas
2–3 tbsp coconut oil

In a large mixing bowl mix the dry ingredients well, and then add the vegetables together so that all is covered with flour and spices.

Now form into golf-size balls and then press flat to form a 'patty', carefully transfer them into the hot coconut oil. Fry until they are golden and crispy on both sides, turning them only once.

Health benefits:

Peas are a good source of plant protein and packed with beneficial fibre. They also contain beta-sitosterol that studies suggest can lower bad cholesterol in the human body. Peas are high in vitamins C and K and B-complex vitamins and phytonutrients like lutein and zea-xanthin.

Sweet potatoes, the orange flesh variety, are one of nature's unsurpassed sources of beta carotene that converts into vitamin A in the body. It is helpful to include some fat with a sweet potato meal as this will increase your body's beta carotene uptake. Sweet potatoes also have anti-inflammatory properties, can assist in curing stomach ulcers and provide relief from arthritis. They are also rich in vitamins C, B1 and B2, a good source of biotin and potassium and an excellent source of fibre.

Gluten & dairy free. Vegan friendly.

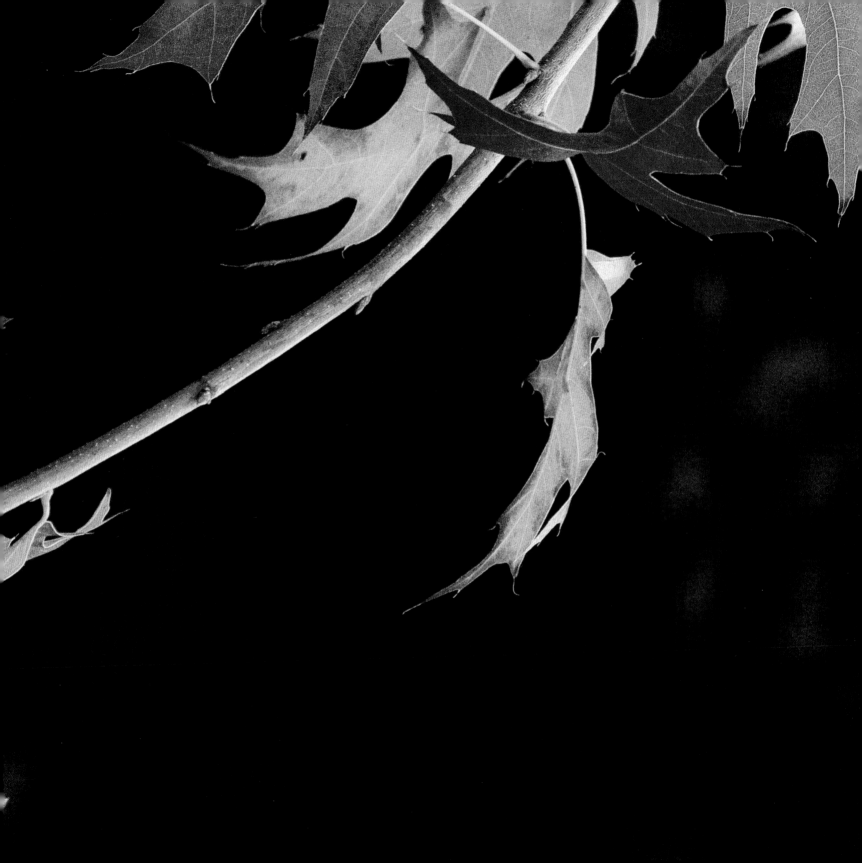

Flexitarian

Food

Superfood Salmon Meal Serves 4

This is such a simple meal that can be put together with hardly any prepping and fuss, but the health benefits are huge. Make sure you use wild-caught not farmed salmon.

4 medium salmon fillets
2 large avocados
12 spears of tender-stem broccoli
Black sesame seeds (optional)
1 tbsp sesame seed oil
1 tbsp tamari sauce
Pink salt

Place the salmon fillets skin down on a baking tray, season them with salt and place them in a preheated 180°C oven for 15–20 minutes.

While the salmon is roasting, prep the avocados by peeling and slicing them. Blanch or flash boil the broccoli spears by submerging them in boiling water and leaving them for 5 minutes to then drain and season with salt.

Combine the sesame oil and tamari sauce. Serve the salmon, broccoli and avocado plated or on a platter with a sprinkle of black sesame seeds and a drizzle of the tamari sauce and sesame oil.

Health benefits

Wild Salmon is super rich in omega-3 fatty acids and a great source of B vitamins, especially B12.

Avocados are truly a superfood. Their health benefits are endless, but to just name a few: they are rich in potassium, folic acid, vitamins E and B, and fibre. They also play an important role in assisting your body to absorb phytonutrients and antioxidants.

Tender-stem broccoli is also classified as a superfood, as it is high in iron and vitamin C, and is full of cancer-fighting phytonutrients and antioxidants, most important of which is sulforaphane, which plays a large role in immune, eye and heart health.

Steak & Homemade Mustard Serves 2

Serve these steak strips with delicious mustard, lambs lettuce & blanched asparagus spears dressed with pink salt & olive oil.

400 g free-range beef rump, or fillet (choose a
    piece that is least 2½ cm thick)
1 tsp coconut oil
1 tsp pink salt

Mustard:
4 tbsp mustard seeds (I use yellow seeds but a
    mixture of yellow & brown works well too)
¼ cup of raw apple cider vinegar
1 tbsp water
1 tbsp honey
1 clove of garlic, crushed
1 tsp pink salt

Simply grind the mustard seeds in a mortar and pestle, or in a spice or coffee grinder, then add the ground mustard seeds together with all the other mustard ingredients into a bowl and mix well until you have a smooth paste, set aside to rest and infuse.

Heat a dry/empty cast iron pan or skillet on high heat for at least 5 minutes until it is piping hot. While the pan is heating, season the steak well with salt and just before placing it in the hot pan add the coconut oil to the pan, making sure it covers the whole base of the pan.

Place the steak into the pan and allow it to cook on high heat for 4 minutes on each side (8 minutes in total). Then remove it from the pan, transferring it to a meat chopping board and allow it to rest for about 8 minutes before slicing it into thin strips with a sharp knife.

Health benefits

Pasture-raised free-range beef is crammed full of highly beneficial omega 3 fatty acids, which is important for brain and skin health, combats inflammation and arthritis and can assist with poor memory or learning difficulties.

Pasture-fed (free-range) beef is also rich in protein, vitamin E, conjugated linoleic acid which exhibits potent antioxidant activity, cartenoids, B-vitamins, vitamin D and iron. As with all foods pasture-fed beef should be eaten in moderation and in conjunction with a balanced diet that includes plenty of vegetables.

Phenolic components in **mustard seeds** offer a magnitude of health benefits such as aiding in alleviating skin disorders like psoriasis, contact dermatitis, and can also contribute to curing bronchitis and other respiratory disorders.

Gluten, grain & dairy free. Paleo friendly.

Pan-fried Hake with Pesto & Cherry Tomatoes Serves 4

This is a gorgeous and delicious summer evening meal that can be thrown together with minimal effort. It goes well with a simple salad of lettuce (they contribute digestive enzymes) and avocado (providing good fats and fibre).

4 large hake fillets (frozen is fine)
250 g punnet of cherry tomatoes
¼ tsp sugar
Salt to season
1 tsp coconut oil

Pesto:
1 cup of fresh coriander leaves
1 cup of rocket leaves
½ cup of raw cashews
75 ml olive oil
Juice of 1 small lemon
1 clove of garlic, grated
Pink salt to taste

Start by making the pesto. Simply add to your blender or food processor all the pesto ingredients and pulse until you have a course, pesto consistency.

Season the fish fillets with salt and place them skin down in a hot skillet/pan with a little coconut oil. They will only need 15 minutes of cooking time, turning them over just once at the very end.

In a separate pan, sauté the cherry tomatoes in a little oil for approximately 5 minutes on high heat, stirring frequently, and season with salt and sugar.

Serve the cooked fillets on a platter, skin down, adding dollops of pesto and the sautéed tomatoes.

Health Benefits

Hake is an excellent source of low fat protein, hake is also packed with other nutrients like vitamin B12, B6, thiamin, riboflavin, folic acid and pantothenic acid. These B vitamins are essential for metabolism and the formation of red blood cells. Hake is also a source of omega 3 fatty acids and minerals such as magnesium, zinc, calcium, selenium and phosphorus.

Coriander, also known as cilantro, is a good source of vitamins K, A and C, folic acid and minerals such as manganese, potassium, copper, iron and calcium. Coriander assists in clearing up skin disorders like eczema and dryness, helps prevent nausea and stomach disorders and helps reduce swelling due to kidney malfunction or anaemia.

Tomatoes are rich in vitamins C and A, both of which fight infections and are essential for immune health. Tomatoes are also high in lycopene, which protects our skin from ultraviolet damage and oxidative stress, as well as reducing the risk of osteoporosis. Try and include cooked tomatoes in your diet frequently, as the lycopene content increases with cooking.

Gluten, grain & dairy free. Paleo friendly.

Prawns & Avocado Boats Serves 4

This makes for a delicious & fragrant starter or light summery supper.

2 tbsp olive oil

2 tbsp teriyaki sauce

¾ tsp salt

⅓ of a red chilli, deseeded and finely chopped

2 large cloves of garlic, finely chopped

Juice of one lime

1 tbsp coconut oil

400 g uncooked, shelled and deveined prawns

6 spring onions, finely chopped

2 large avocados, pitted and cut in half

In a bowl, mix the olive oil, teriyaki sauce, salt, chilli, garlic and lime juice well and set aside to infuse.

Heat a large and deep cast-iron pan. When the pan is very hot add the coconut oil, and sauté the prawns and spring onions for approximately 4 minutes on high heat.

After 4 minutes transfer the cooked prawns and spring onions into the bowl with the teriyaki sauce and toss the prawns through the sauce.

Serve plated, over half a ripe avocado.

Health benefits

Prawns are a good source of protein, vitamins A and E, and minerals such as calcium, potassium and phosphorus, but eat them in moderation as they are also high in cholesterol.

Avocados are truly a superfood. Their health benefits are endless, but to just name a few: they are rich in potassium, folic acid, vitamin E and B, and fibre. They also play an important role in assisting your body to absorb phytonutrients and antioxidants.

Paleo Chicken & Vegetable Roast Serves 4

4 each free-range chicken thighs and
drumsticks

Pink salt to taste

Black pepper to taste

4 fennel bulbs, stems and leaves removed

4 cloves of garlic with the skin on

2 red onions, chopped into rough quarters

2–3 large carrots, peeled and sliced thickly
diagonally

1 sprig each of thyme and rosemary

12 spears of asparagus

Preheat the oven to 180°C, then spread the chicken pieces
evenly in a large roasting pan. Season with salt and black pepper
and transfer to the oven, letting it roast for approximately 25
minutes.

After 25 minutes add the whole fennel bulbs, unpeeled garlic,
onions, carrots and herbs. Season the vegetables with salt and
then put them back into the oven for a further 35 minutes, adding
the asparagus 10 minutes before the end of the total roasting
time.

Serve with a green salad.

Health benefits

Asparagus contains significant quantities of the nutrient inulin which is a complex prebiotic that only starts getting digested when it reaches the large intestine where it is fed upon by good bacteria like lactobacilli, which aids in improved absorption of nutrients and reduced risk of stomach cancer and allergies. Asparagus also helps to elevate levels of glutathione, an antioxidant and detoxifying compound which plays a major role in aging and helps prevent illnesses like cystic fibroses, Alzheimer's disease, anaemia and cancer. Asparagus can also assist with alleviating PMS bloating and is especially beneficial to pregnant women as it is very high in folic acid. Fun fact: asparagus is a great for curing a hangover due to its liver cleansing properties.

Fennel is effective in relieving indigestion, bad breath and flatulence. It is also rich in vitamins C and A, folic acid and niacin, and minerals such as potassium, magnesium, calcium and iron. Fennel is also helpful in regulating hormones and the menstrual cycle, as well as being a relaxing agent during menopause.

Gluten, grain & dairy free. Paleo friendly.

Greek Lamb Chops with Tzatziki & Greens Serves 4

This is a great dish for a dinner or lunch party; the chops can also be done on the barbeque. I often add roasted aubergine wedges to this meal.

8–12 lamb cutlets

150 g fine 'French' green beans, topped & tailed

Watercress (110g packet/ bunch should do)

300 ml Greek yoghurt

2 tsp dried dill

2 cloves of garlic, crushed

Juice of 2 medium lemons

Zest of a lemon

1 tbsp olive oil

2 sprigs of thyme, leaves stripped

Salt to taste

Roasted pine nuts to garnish (optional)

Place the lamb in an oven-proof dish to marinate. Dress the cutlets with the olive oil, thyme, salt, one clove of crushed garlic, the lemon juice and 1 tablespoon of lemon zest. Toss the cutlets through this marinade, cover the dish and let it marinade at room temperature for approximately 30 minutes.

In a separate bowl, add the Greek yoghurt, second clove of crushed garlic, a teaspoon of lemon zest, dill, and salt to taste. Stir well and set aside to infuse.

Pop the cutlets into a preheated oven at 200°C for 15–20 minutes. While the cutlets are baking, blanch the green beans for 3 minutes in boiling water, draining them well and season with pink salt and a drizzle of olive oil.

Prepare a serving platter laid out with the watercress and green beans. Place the lamb cutlets on top of the greens, drizzle with olive oil, and serve with dollops of tzatziki here and there.

Health benefits

Free-range lamb is rich in omega-3 fatty acids and conjugated linoleic acid (CLA content), a type of fat that has anti-cancer and heart health benefits. Of course the protein content in this meat is exceptional, with is also rich in vitamin B12, zinc and selenium.

Green beans are rich in a wide variety of vitamins and minerals as well as omega-3 fatty acids and many different phytonutrients that have all been shown to have heart-health-supportive antioxidant properties. The fibre content is also impressive and since they are so tasty and easy to prepare they are a great addition to your diet on a regular basis. Add them to stews, salads and Thai curries.

Mackerel Fishcakes with Tangy Slaw Serves 4

Fishcakes:

2–3 large smoked mackerel fillets
1 free-range egg
½ small red onion, chopped fine
¼ cup of fresh parsley, chopped fine
1 tsp pink salt

3 tbsp coconut oil

Slaw:

2 carrots
1 baby white cabbage
4 radishes (optional)
½ small red onion
2 tbsp mayonnaise (use a non-tangy brand)
1 tbsp Dijon mustard
Juice of half a small lemon
1 tbsp honey
Salt to taste
Ground black pepper to taste

De-bone and remove the fish fillets' skin, or even better ask your fishmonger to prep them for you. Chop the fish into large chunks, placing it into a food processor along with all the other fishcake ingredients. Pulse until you have a course mixture that can be formed into small fishcakes of approximately 5 cm in diameter, and 2 cm thick. Shallow fry these lovely little fishcakes in the coconut oil. They should be crispy and golden on both sides.

Shred the carrots, cabbage and radishes, and slice the red onion finely. Add to a bowl and then mix well together with the mayonnaise, mustard, lemon juice, honey, salt and pepper.

Health benefits

Mackerel is extremely high in omega-3 fatty acids that protect against heart disease, prostate cancer and dementia, to name just a few. Mackerel is also an excellent source of protein, vitamin D, B vitamins and selenium.

Paleo friendly, gluten & grain free.

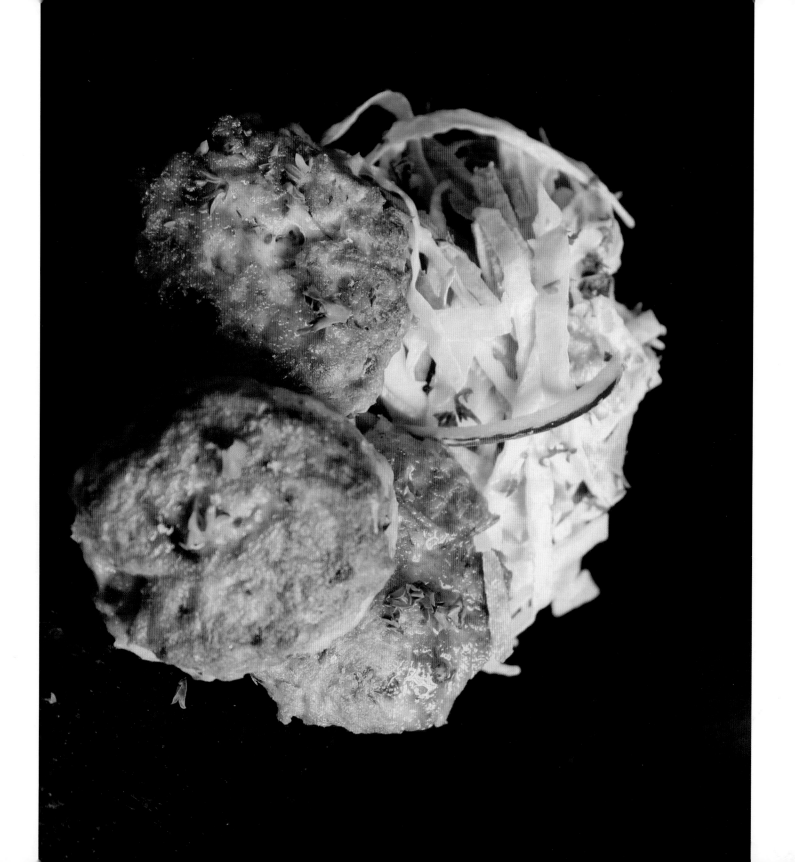

Chicken & Veggie Skewers with Spicy Peanut Sauce Serves 4

These skewers are also perfect for the barbeque.

8 de-boned & skinless chicken thighs (free-range or organic)
1 large red pepper, chopped into 2½ cm squares)
2 red onions, hopped into 2½ cm squares)
250 g punnet of white mushrooms, stems removed
2 tbsp sesame oil
8 long bamboo skewers
A generous grinding of pink salt

Spicy Peanut Sauce to serve (see page 36)
Asian 'Crunch' Salad to serve (see page 48)

Cut the chicken into large cubes. Assemble your skewers in evenly mixed 'rainbow' layers, alternating between the meat and the different vegetables. When they have all been used up, season them with salt and a drizzle of oil, then pop them in a preheated 180°C oven and let them roast for approximately 30 minutes.

Serve these delicious skewers with a generous drizzle of the Spicy Peanut Sauce and a portion of the salad.

Health benefits

Free-range/organic (or pasture-raised) chicken is an excellent source of protein, vitamins B12 and E, zinc and selenium. Vitamin B12 is only available from animal products like meat and dairy, and fulfils hugely important roles in the body like helping the blood carry oxygen, which is essential for energy production and is extremely important for nerve function.

Yoga Kitchen Lamb Curry Serves 6–8

To keep within the food-combining rules, serve on cauliflower 'rice' – steam or boil a head of cauliflower in salted water, then crumble with a masher or a fork until it resembles cooked rice kernels. This way, you add another vegetable to your meal within the food-combining rules.

3 red onions

Coconut oil or ghee

2 tsp turmeric

1 tsp coriander powder

1 tsp sweet paprika

½ tsp chilli powder

1 tbsp garam masala

1 tbsp cumin seeds

1 tsp mustard seeds

1 tsp fennel seeds

½ tsp allspice

2 bay leaves

2 whole cloves

2 green cardamom pods

600 g free-range lamb knuckles

4 2½ cm of pasture-raised, beef shin bones

4 cloves of garlic, finely grated

2 tbsp fresh ginger, grated

1 400 ml tin of coconut cream

300 ml of passata

or 8 large tomatoes, chopped

200 ml water

Pink salt to taste

Fresh coriander leaves for garnishing

1 medium head of cauliflower for the 'cauli-rice'

Finely chop and fry the onions in coconut oil or ghee until they are soft and golden.

Next add the spices, garlic and ginger, and fry on low heat all together for another 5 minutes.

Add the lamb knuckles and beef shin bones, browning and stirring occasionally for approximately 7 minutes.

Lastly, add the passata, or chopped tomatoes, coconut cream, salt and water, letting it cook over low heat, with the lid on, for 2 hours, stirring every 30 minutes or so. Garnish with chopped coriander, and serve.

Health benefits

Free-range lamb is rich in omega-3 fatty acids and greater conjugated linoleic acid, or CLA content, a type of fat that has anti-cancer and heart-health benefits. Of course the protein content is exceptional and lamb is also rich in vitamin B12, zinc and selenium.

Curcumin in **turmeric** is a superfood. It encourages the gallbladder to produce bile which improves digestion, is a powerful anti-inflammatory and can help diminish the symptoms of osteoarthritis and rheumatic conditions. Turmeric can assist in preventing a number of cancers including breast, colon, prostrate and skin.

Garlic protects against stomach cancer, lowers cholesterol in the blood, helps to prevent blood clots and is an excellent immune booster.

Mandarin Chicken Stir-fry Serves 4

I like to add a teaspoon of miso paste mixed with a little cold-pressed sesame oil before serving (sparing it the high heat). Miso is filled with probiotics and other beneficial minerals and adds a delicious flavour.

Coconut oil

4 free-range chicken breast fillets, cut into
1½-cm-thick strips

Pink salt to taste

2 tbsps tamari or soy sauce

1 baby green cabbages, chopped and
shredded

6 spears of spring onion, roughly chopped

3 medium carrots, peeled and grated

10 spears of tender-stem broccoli, roughly
chopped

1 tbsp ginger, finely grated

1 tbsp garlic, finely grated

1 tbsp fish sauce

Black sesame seeds (optional)

Sesame oil and miso paste for drizzling before
serving (optional)

Heat a wok or cast-iron pan/skillet until it is piping hot, then add the coconut oil and make sure it covers the base of the pan. Next add the chicken breast strips, season with salt and a tablespoon of soy sauce. Do not stir, just let the strips cook on high heat and turn them after approximately 3 minutes. This way the strips stay soft and juicy, but have a lovely golden colour as well.

Once the strips are cooked, transfer them to a bowl to rest. Then using the same wok or skillet, add all of the vegetables, ginger, garlic, salt, fish sauce and tamari sauce, stir-frying them all together for 10–12 minutes on medium heat. Lastly, add the chicken again for a minute or less to reheat and serve with a sprinkling of toasted white sesame seeds and black sesame seeds (optional).

Health benefits

Free-range chicken is an excellent source of protein, vitamins B12 and E, zinc and selenium. It really is worth buying free-range or organic chicken instead of commercially farmed chicken that contain toxins like antibiotics and hormones which wreck havoc on your health.

Cabbage is a powerhouse of vitamins and antioxidants, especially vitamin C. Cabbage is a good source of minerals such as manganese and potassium, and is abundant in important phytonutrients and polyphenols that fight cancer. What makes cabbage even more beneficial to your health is the impressive fibre that prevents constipation and helps bind bile acids in the stomach.

Gluten, grain & dairy free. Paleo friendly.

Bazaar Ground Beef Curry Serves 4–6

This is my version of the classic South African bazaar curry. Traditionally eaten with vetkoek or yellow rice, it should be served with some cauli-rice if you want to stick to the food-combining rules. See the Yoga Kitchen Lamb Curry on page xxx to see how to cook cauli-rice. I have also added coconut milk which you wouldn't add traditionally to this curry, but makes it so delicious.

2 medium brown or yellow onions
1 tbsp coconut oil
2 cloves of garlic
1 tsp mustard seeds
1 tsp cumin seeds
3 bay leaves
1 tsp ground cumin
½ tsp allspice
1 tbsp ground coriander
1 tbsp turmeric
1 tbsp garam masala
1 tsp ground black pepper
500 g free-range or organic ground beef
1 cup of carrot, grated
Pink salt to taste
1 400 g tin of coconut milk or cream
1 cup of spinach, chopped, tightly packed
Chopped coriander to garnish (optional)

Cook onions in the coconut oil until they are soft and golden. Add the minced garlic, as well as all the spices, frying for a further 3 minutes on low heat.

Add the ground beef, carrot and salt. Separate the ground beef with a fork, stirring continuously while the beef is browning.

Next add the coconut cream/milk, and stir through before turning the heat down and placing the lid on the pot to let it simmer slowly for another 25 minutes.

Lastly, add the spinach approximately 5 minutes before serving; it only needs to 'wilt' and heat through.

Health benefits

Pasture-raised, free-range or organic beef is crammed full of highly beneficial omega-3 fatty acids, which is important for brain and skin health, combats inflammation and arthritis, and can assist with poor memory or learning difficulties. Free-range beef is also rich in protein, vitamin E, conjugated linoleic acid, which exhibits potent antioxidant activity, cartenoids, B vitamins, vitamin D and iron. As with all foods, beef should be eaten in moderation and in conjunction with a balanced diet that includes plenty of vegetables.

Gluten & grain free & dairy free. Paleo friendly.

Middle Eastern Stuffed Aubergines with Lamb and Pine Nuts Serves 4

300 g free-range ground lamb
2 large aubergines, halved
2 tsp sweet paprika
2 tsp ground cumin
1 tsp freshly ground black pepper
1 tsp ground coriander
½ tsp cinnamon
½ tsp ground nutmeg
¼ tsp cloves
1 tsp pink salt
¼ cup of pine nuts
1 tsp coconut oil

Sauce:
2 tbsp tahini paste
2 tbsp water
¼ tsp cumin
¼ tsp paprika
1 clove of garlic, crushed

Whisk all the sauce ingredients together and set aside to infuse.

Start by hollowing out the centres of the aubergines (take about 4 tablespoons of the flesh of each half, discard, or roast seperately and add the soft, roasted flesh to the lamb mixture before stuffing). Then rub the hollowed out insides with coconut oil and season with salt. Place them skin down in a 170°C preheated oven for approximately 40–50 minutes.

While the aubergines are roasting, start frying the lamb mince in a deep pan or skillet and when it starts browning, add the spices, stirring and separating the ground lamb with a fork continuously until all the lamb is crumbly and cooked through (it needs approximately 15–20 minutes).

Then add the pine nuts to a dry pan and lightly toast them for about 3–5 minutes on medium heat, stirring and shaking frequently.

When the aubergines are ready (their flesh should cooked through to silky soft), remove them from the oven and scoop into each half equal portions of spiced lamb, sprinkle over the lightly toasted pine nuts and then drizzle over the garlicky tahini sauce and serve with a green salad.

Health benefits

Free-range lamb is rich in omega-3 fatty acids and also greater conjugated linoleic acid, or CLA content, a type of fat that has anti-cancer and heart-health benefits. The protein content in lamb is exceptional with it also being rich in vitamin B12, zinc and selenium.

Aubergines, also known as eggplant or brinjal, have an impressive spectrum of nutrients in them, fibre: folic acid, potassium, manganese, as well as vitamins C, K and B6, phosphorous, copper, thiamine, niacin, magnesium and pantothenic acid. The phytonutrient nasunin, found in the skin of aubergine, is a powerful antioxidant that protects brain cells against free radical damage.

Carb-free Bacon & Spinach Tart Serves 4–6

250 g naturally smoked, free-range, streaky bacon

1 tbsp of coconut oil or butter

1 red onion, sliced finely

2 cups baby spinach, finely shredded or chopped

2 large free-range eggs

1 cup of Greek yoghurt

Pink salt and black pepper to taste

½ cup of gruyere or cheddar cheese, finely grated

Place the bacon in individually laid out strips on a dripping rack in a 180°C preheated oven for 15–20 minutes. I like to crisp the fat before removing it to cool.

In the coconut oil, sauté the onions on low heat until they are soft and translucent, then add the baby spinach and sauté until it has become completely 'wilted'.

Once the bacon is crispy, remove it from the oven to cool, but keep the oven on for later use. Once the bacon is cool enough to handle, use scissors to cut it into small strips.

In a mixing bowl whisk the eggs together with the yoghurt, then add the salt and pepper, next the grated cheese, chopped bacon and finally the sautéed spinach.

Now pour the mixture into a deep, greased baking tin or oven-proof dish and place it in the oven for 20–25 minutes. Remove and serve with a fresh green salad.

Health benefits

Make sure you purchase your **free-range**, or even better **organic**, **bacon** from a reputable butcher, market or store. Choosing 'naturally smoked' is also essential. The most important health benefits of free-range or pasture-fed pork come from the abundance of omega-3 & -6 fatty acids in its fat. It is worth storing the drippings from your free-range pork to roast vegetables in, not only for the great flavour but also for its contribution to the nutrition of the vegetables. Free-range/organic pork is free from antibiotics, high in protein and an excellent source of saturated fats, which we now know are essential for the correct functioning of our brain. As with everything, pork fat should be consumed in moderation.

Spinach is rich in vitamins A, C, E and K and minerals such as zinc, iron, magnesium, phosphorus, potassium, copper and manganese. It is full of nutrition and fibre and worth eating often. I often use raw spinach instead of salad leaves in my salads.

Smoked Salmon & Broccoli Quiche Serves 4

4 eggs

pink salt & black pepper to taste

1 cup of Greek yoghurt

½ cup of smoked salmon, sliced into strips

½ cup of cheddar cheese

8 fine spears of tender-stem broccoli, blanched

Preheat the oven to 180°C.

In a mixing bowl, whisk the eggs and Greek yoghurt well, then season with salt and black pepper. Stir through the grated cheese and sliced salmon.

Grease a fairly deep baking tin with butter and pour in the egg mixture. Decorate the top with the broccoli spears, pushing them down gently into the mixture.

Bake for 30 minutes, then remove and allow to cool for a couple of minutes before serving with a fresh leafy green salad.

Health benefits

Wild salmon is very rich in omega-3 fatty acids and a great source of B vitamins, especially B12.

Tender-stem broccoli is high in iron, vitamin C and cancer-fighting phytonutrients and antioxidants, especially sulforaphane, which plays an important role in immune, eye and heart health.

Sweet Surrender

Raw Chocolate Mousse Serves 4–6

3 medium, ripe avocados

⅓ cup of real maple syrup or coconut sugar

2 very ripe bananas

½ cup of cashew butter

½ cup of raw cacao powder

1 tsp of vanilla extract

Add all the ingredients to your high speed blender, or food processor, and whiz until you have a smooth mixture (you should stop every other minute or so to scrape the sides).

Transfer the delightfully creamy chocolate mixture to the fridge for 2 hours to chill, and serve it with some fresh berries – raspberries, blackberries or strawberries are great choices.

Health benefits

Raw cacao powder is classified as a superfood due to the wealth of antioxidants, vitamins and minerals it contains. It is worth highlighting the amazing antioxidant power of cacao beans that include improving heart health, fighting cancer and mood enhancement. Make sure you select RAW cacao powder from your local health store, which means the cacao beans have not been roasted. When the beans are roasted they are stripped of all their antioxidants. Cacao does contain caffeine and so should eat it in moderation.

Avocados provide good fats and fibre like vitamin E, folic acid and antioxidants.

Cashews are high in magnesium, a mineral which most people are deficient in due to large-scale farming. Magnesium is involved in over 200 functions in our bodies. Cashews also contain vitamin E, copper, selenium and healthy fats.

Gluten, grain & dairy free. Vegan & paleo friendly.

Pecan & Maple Nice Cream Serves 4

3 large ripe bananas

½ cup of cashew or almond butter

½ cup of maple syrup

¼ cup of tahini

Pinch of salt

2 tsp pure vanilla extract,
or the seeds of a vanilla pod scraped out

1 cup of raw pecans, crushed

Place all the ingredients except for the pecans in your food processor, then blitz them into a smooth cream. Add the crushed pecans and give it a gentle stir.

Place the nice cream into an airtight plastic container, pop it into the freezer for at least 4–6 hours. Take it out 10 minutes before serving to soften.

Gluten, grain & dairy free. Paleo & vegan friendly.

Blackberry & Banana Nice Cream Serves 4

3 ripe bananas

¼ cup of raw honey

¾ cup of blackberries (fresh or frozen)

1 cup of coconut cream, whipped

In a food processor or a high speed blender, process the banana, honey and blackberries until you have a smooth, creamy mixture and then fold it into whipped coconut cream, being careful to keep the air bubbles. It looks lovely when you can see the swirls of white and dark red, so there is no need to mix it too well.

Transfer it to an airtight plastic container and freeze for 4–6 hours. Remove the container from the freezer 5–10 minutes before serving to soften.

Gluten, grain & dairy free. Paleo friendly and vegan friendly, if you replace the honey with real maple syrup.

Health benefits

Bananas can provide relief from constipation, assist with eye and bone health, and reduce inflammation from gout and arthritis. Bananas soothe an upset stomach and reduce acid secretion. The organic compounds in bananas stimulate the activity of the cells in our stomach lining to build up a protective barrier against acids. Bananas are rich in vitamin B6 and potassium.

Blackberries are very rich in antioxidants which can reduce DNA damage by free radicals. Blackberries are power houses of phytonutrients that fight cancer and can even inhibit tumour growth. Blackberries are immune boosters due to their high vitamin C content, as well as bone builders because of their magnesium, calcium and phosphorus content. They also contribute to skin health as they have both vitamin C and vitamin E in abundance.

Pecans are abundant in antioxidants, especially in the brown skin around the nut. They also assist in maintaining a healthy cholesterol balance in the body and are rich in vitamin E, thiamine, B6 and panthogenic acid and minerals such as manganese, magnesium, copper and zinc.

Raw Cashew Butter Brownies

Peanut butter can be substituted for the cashew butter, but make sure it is non-GMO.

I prefer the walnuts to be soaked overnight, dried and then lightly roasted (7 minutes in a 150°C preheated oven) before using them to garnish the brownies.

¾ cup of cashew butter

1 cup of medjool dates

2 tbsp coconut oil

2 tbsp honey

100 g good quality, 85%-cocoa, dark chocolate

Pinch of fine pink salt

10 walnuts or pecans to garnish

Melt the dark chocolate over low heat in a heat-proof bowl.

Pour the melted chocolate, along with all the other ingredients, into your food processor and blend until you have a smooth mixture.

Transfer the mixture to a spring-form cake tin, garnish the top with some halved walnuts or pecans and then pop it in the freezer for 1 hour. Next, transfer the tin to the fridge until fully set. It will last well in the fridge for at least a week (although it never has the opportunity to in our house!).

Health benefits

The high fibre content in **medjool dates** helps to move waste smoothly through the colon and helps prevent bad cholesterol. Dates are also rich in iron, potassium, B vitamins, vitamins A and K, as well as minerals such as copper and magnesium.

85% dark chocolate is full of important antioxidants and polyphenols, and is rated as a superfood due to its anti-inflammatory and antioxidant properties. Good quality dark chocolate can play an important role in lowering your risk of many diseases like Alzheimer's, diabetes, heart disease, cancer, preeclampsia in pregnant women and cirrhosis.

Gluten, grain & dairy free. Vegan & paleo friendly.

Naked Baklava & Greek Yoghurt Serves 6–8

½ cup of almonds

½ cup of walnuts

¼ cup of unsalted pistachios, shelled

⅓ cup of butter, melted

⅓ cup of raw honey

1½ tsp cinnamon

½ tsp ground cloves

Greek yoghurt to serve

Preheat your oven to 150°C, then place the nuts on a clean baking tray and allow them to roast for 5–7 minutes. Remove and, after cooling them for a few minutes, transfer them to your food processor and then blitz them very briefly until you have a broken-nut mixture that you then pour into a large mixing bowl.

Now add the butter, honey and spices to the nuts and mix well until all of the nuts are coated. Transfer the bowl to the fridge to cool for 30 minutes before serving with full fat Greek yoghurt.

Health benefits

Almonds are rich in vitamin E, omega-3 fatty acids, protein, manganese, zinc and calcium. I recommend soaking almonds overnight before use as this deactivates the enzyme-inhibiting compound found in their skin.

Walnuts can help reduce bad cholesterol, improve metabolism and aid in weight management. They also possess anti-inflammatory properties and can be a mood booster. Walnuts are also a great source of omega-3 fatty acids.

Gluten & grain free. Paleo friendly.

Flourless Lemon Zest & Almond Torte Serves 6–8

4 eggs, separated into 4 yolks & 4 whites
(eggs must be room temperature)
½ cup of golden castor sugar
1 heaped tbsp lemon zest
1½ cups of fine almond flour
1 tsp baking soda
½ tsp pink salt
½ cup of unsalted butter, melted
Almond slivers for garnishing, lightly toasted
Icing sugar to dust and serve

Preheat the oven to 150°C.

With a hand mixer, beat the egg whites until they form soft peaks.

In a separate bowl, beat the egg yolks, castor sugar, lemon zest, almond flour, baking soda, salt and cooled butter together.

Then fold in the egg whites, taking care to preserve the air bubbles. Transfer the mixture to a greased or lined 23-cm spring-form tin.

Bake for 30–35 minutes; the top should be golden brown.

Remove to cool fully before garnishing with the almond slivers and a dusting of icing sugar before serving.

Health benefits

Almond flour is grain and gluten free, low in carbohydrates and a good source of protein.

Gluten & grain free. Can be dairy free and vegan friendly, if the butter is replaced with coconut oil.

Flourless Chocolate Torte Serves 8

4 eggs, separated into 4 yolks & 4 whites, at room temperature

⅓ cup of golden castor sugar

1½ cups of fine almond flour

1 tsp baking soda

½ tsp pink salt

½ cup of unsalted butter, melted

200 g 85%-cocoa dark chocolate, melted gently

Cacao or cocoa powder for dusting

Preheat the oven to 170°C.

With a hand mixer, beat the egg whites until they form soft peaks.

In a separate bowl, beat the egg yolks, castor sugar, almond flour, baking soda, salt cooled butter and chocolate together.

Fold in the egg whites carefully, taking care to preserve the air bubbles and transfer the mixture to a greased or lined 23-cm spring-form tin.

Bake the torte for 30–35 minutes, remove and allow it to cool before serving with some chocolate powder dusted on top.

Health benefits

Almond flour is grain and gluten free, low in carbohydrates and a good source of protein.

85% dark chocolate is crammed full of antioxidants. It is worth highlighting its amazing antioxidant effects on heart health, fighting cancer and mood enhancement.

Gluten & grain free. Paleo friendly. Can be dairy free and vegan friendly if the butter is replaced with coconut oil.

Chia Pudding Serves 4–6

3 cups of unsweetened almond milk
½ cup of chia seeds
3 tbsp real maple syrup
1 tsp vanilla extract
Fresh fruit and nuts to serve

Whisk all the ingredients together in a bowl and then allow it to sit for about 10 minutes. Then whisk the mixture again to avoid clumps.

Next transfer it to the fridge for 2 hours and then serve the pudding with fresh fruit and lightly toasted nuts (almonds and cashews work well).

Health benefits

Chia seeds are the single richest plant-based source of omega-3 fatty acids. Chia seeds are also loaded with protein, antioxidants and minerals.

Grain, gluten & dairy free. Vegan & paleo friendly.

Date & Coconut Protein Balls Makes 10 balls

This healthy treat is free from refined sugars, packed with fibre and a good helping of healthy fats as well as protein. They are a great addition to lunch boxes or can be served successfully as a healthy party treat.

½ cup of pitted medjool dates
½ cup of coconut flour
½ cup of smooth peanut butter
2 tbsp chia seeds
2 tbsp honey
¼ cup of desiccated coconut
Pinch of pink salt

Simply add all the ingredients to your food processor, and then whiz it together, giving your machine a break every minute or so until you have a sticky dough consistency (it doesn't need to be 100% smooth).

Then use your hands to shape the 'dough' into ping-pong-sized balls. Roll them through the desiccated coconut and then serve, or store them in a cling-film-covered dish in the fridge. Use within 3–4 days.

Health benefits

The high fibre content in **dates** helps to move waste smoothly through the colon and helps prevent bad cholesterol. Dates are also rich in iron, potassium, B vitamins, vitamins A and K, as well as minerals such as copper and magnesium.

Chia seeds are an excellent source of plant-based omega-3 fatty acids and plant protein.

Peanut butter contains vitamin E and is a good source of plant protein.

Desiccated coconut is an excellent source of fibre.

Gluten, grain & dairy free. Vegan friendly.

Luxurious Vegan Hot Chocolate Makes 2 cups

½ cup of coconut cream
1 cup of almond milk
2 tsp Demerara sugar
2 tbsp cacao powder
A tiny pinch of nutmeg

Combine all the ingredients (holding two teaspoons of coconut cream back) in a deep saucepan and bring it to almost boiling point, whisking and stirring continuously.
Serve hot with a tablespoon of coconut cream on top.

Health benefits

Cacao is rich in antioxidants and polyphenols, and is rated as a superfood due to its anti-inflammatory and antioxidant properties. Cacao can play an important role in lowering your risk of many diseases like Alzheimer's, diabetes, heart disease, cancer, preeclampsia in pregnant women and cirrhosis.

Turmeric Chai

Makes 2 large cups

1–2 rooibos tea bags
50 ml boiling water
½ tsp turmeric
1 small thumb-sized piece of ginger
1 stick of cinnamon, grated
1 clove (optional)
2 cloves (optional)
2 cups of almond milk
1 tbsp coconut oil

Boil the water and submerge the tea bags in it, letting it steep for at least 10 minutes. Remove the tea bags, squeezing all the moisture out and transfer the tea to a deep sauce pan.

Add all the other ingredients to the saucepan and, while stirring continuously, bring it to boiling point. At this stage, remove it from the heat, strain through a fine sieve and serve.

Health benefits

Curcumin in **turmeric** is a superfood, which encourages the gallbladder to produce bile which improves digestion. It is a powerful anti-inflammatory and can help diminish the symptoms of osteoarthritis and rheumatic conditions. Turmeric can assist in preventing a number of cancers including breast, colon, prostrate and skin.

171

About the author

Marlien Wright is a teacher of yoga and Pilates, a certified nutritional therapy coach, a mum, country dweller, former city girl, and a part-time hippy. She's been studying movement, holistic wellness and nutrition as long as anyone can remember.

Her love of good food ignited while she was travelling and living abroad, where she discovered all the weird and wonderful foods out there and felt inspired to recreate them in her own kitchen.

Marlien's Yoga Kitchen journey began when she started hosting and blogging about her country yoga retreats, endeavouring to create nourishing retreat meals that are simple, and promote healing and radiant health. Marlien is passionate about nutrition and helping others rediscover their best health.

For more information on Marlien's yoga, cooking and nutrition retreats, visit www.yogakitchen.co.za.

Index

Pages numbers in bold indicate where the health benefits for each entry are given.